SELECTED SPEECHES
──────────────── VOLUME 5

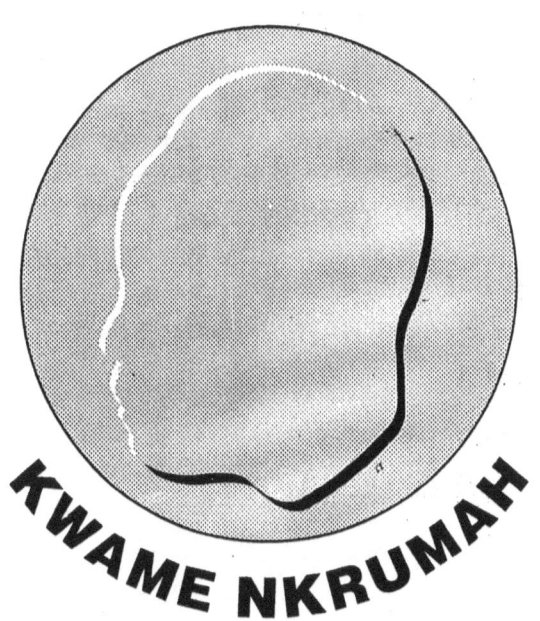

KWAME NKRUMAH

Compiled by Samuel Obeng

AFRAM PUBLICATIONS (GHANA) LTD.

Published by:

Afram Publications (Ghana) Ltd.
P. O. Box M. 18,
Accra, Ghana

© **The Republic of Ghana, 1960**

All Rights Reserved. No part of this book may be reprinted, or reproduced or utilized in any form or by any electronic, invented or other means, now known, including photocopying or recording, or any information storage and retrieval system, without permission in writing from Afram Publications (Ghana) Limited.

First Published 1997

ISBN 9964 70 205 1

Typeset by Damana Graphics

Printed by **Sakoa Press Limited,**

FOREWORD

In the very first Volume of these Works published in 1973 it was suggested that, that Dr. Kwame Nkrumah, "a man who was (in his lifetime) so maligned, condemned and rejected by his own people should at his death be praised and loved so much and be finally accepted by his own people again, appears to testify to Nkrumah's charisma." This proposition has since it was made assumed greater significance in the light of later developments.

Since Dr. Kwame Nkrumah's death the Nkrumah factor has been very forcefully projected in politics and even in the daily lives of the people of Ghana and Africa. Nkrumah's influence has dominated the conduct of the majority of political parties in Ghana. These parties have all laid claim to descent from Dr. Kwame Nkrumah's Convention People's Party and to the Nkrumahist ideology.

Over the period Dr. Nkrumah's statute which was "brutalised" and shoved into obscurity has been re-created and displayed at the Mausoleum built for him in Accra. Furthermore his mortal remains have been transferred from his lowly Nkroful hometown and re-interred at this Mausoleum built and named after him at the very grounds in Accra where he proclaimed independence status for the then Gold Coast forty years ago.

Dr. Nkrumah was concerned with the unity and development of the whole of Ghana. He was concerned with the total welfare of its citizens; his was a vision of a welfare society where all in Ghana would enjoy a reasonably improved standard of life, hence his emphasis on the provision of social amenities like, health, and education. By this strategy he hoped to achieve accelerated economic development.

Nkrumah was passionately committed to the total liberation of the African continent and its eventual unity.

These concerns for domestic and international harmony and development are reflected in all his speeches, short and long, delivered at home and at numerous international fora. Some of the issues he addressed have over the years been resolved; but others like stability in Africa, improved social facilities for Ghana are still relevant.

When one talks of the indestructibility of the tongue it is in reference to the spoken word. In Dr. Kwame Nkrumah's speeches one finds this clearly illustrated. Hardly a national celebration passes without a reminder of Kwame's famous old Polo Grounds Speech declaring Ghana's Independence.

These volume of "Selected Speeches of Dr. Kwame Nkrumah" comes in the fortieth year of Ghana's Independence. It is hoped that the work will urge Ghanaians and friends of Ghana to push ahead with the principles and ideals which some fifty years and more ago inspired the struggle to build Ghana into a "middle level economy."

Accra
August, 1997

William Yaw Eduful
(Publicity Director)
Publicity Secretariate,
Flagstaff House, Accra.

PREFACE

Osagyefo Dr. Kwame Nkrumah had always been in the vanguard of what he himself called "The African Revolution." He had not only been at the centre of its political action, but had also articulated its ideology.

After Dr. Nkrumah's Government was overthrown by a military coup d' etat, on February 24, 1966, he was so much maligned, condemned and rejected by his own people that his books, speeches and pictures that could be reached were publicly burnt.

One afternoon in August, 1971 when I heard a news broadcast on Ghana Broadcasting Corporation Radio that an Act 380 of 28th August, 1971, had banned the use of any slogan by word or shiboleth, photograph, or policy document intended to revive the Convention People's Party (CPP) or its leader or chairman Dr. Kwame Nkrumah, I decided to gather the speeches from those who had them.

I wrote to the Government of the National Redemption Council when the obnoxious Act 380 of August, 1971 was repealed by NRCD 21 of 9th February, 1972, and was given a written permission to compile and publish the Speeches of Kwame Nkrumah.

Kwame Nkrumah's speeches, most of which are being presented together to the world in these volumes, still glow with the force of his personality, his conviction in the face of powerful opposition, his originality, his vision as well as his impatience when his expectations seemed delaying.

Nkrumah did not live to see all his dreams realised, but in his speeches and writings, he has left for posterity ideas which should inspire Africans and Black people everywhere.

It is my hope that readers of these volumes and future generations will derive from these pages the inspiration to fight to uproot the remnants of colonialism from the society.

Samuel Obeng
Compiler

Kumasi,
August, 1997

Dedicated to
politicians and Ex-servicemen
and Brothers and Sisters in the Diaspora
who laid down their lives
to make Ghana's Independence possible

"Truth forever on the scaffold,
Wrong forever on the throne
Yet that scaffold sways the future,
And, behind the dim unknown,
Standeth God within the shadow,
Keeping watch above his own."

—*James Russel Lowell*

CONTENTS

1. 13th Anniversary of the Declaration of Positive Action..................1
2. Official Opening of Kwame Nkrumah Market..............................4
3. Dinner with Businessmen..6
4. University Dinner..10
5. On the Eve of 6th Independence Anniversary.............................15
6. Sixth Independence Anniversary Diplomatic Dinner....................17
7. Volta River Project..20
8. World Youth Day..25
9. May Day Broadcast..26
10. Conference of African Heads of State and Government............30
11. Closing Remarks after Signing of O. A. U. Charter....................47
12. On Arrival at Accra Airport...49
13. Third Anniversary of Ghana Young Pioneers.............................51
14. Fourth Anniversary of the Convention People's Party.................53
15. Ratification of the O. A. U. Charter..................................57
16. Opening of Government House...76
17. Opening of the Unilever Soap Factory..................................79
18. Tribute to Dr. W. E. B. Du Bois.......................................87
19. National Founder's Day..89
20. Ghana Military Academy Passing-out Parade.............................90
21. Sessional Review of the Third Session of the First Parliament Of The Republic of Ghana..................................93
22. Tenth Anniversary of the United Ghana Farmers' Council Co-operatives..104
23. Formal Opening of the Oil Refinery...................................107
24. Opening of the National Assembly.....................................111
25. United Nations Day...126
26. Opening of the Institute of African Studies..........................127
27. Opening of the Second Conference of African Journalists..........140
28. Tribute to the Late President John F. Kennedy........................158
29. The Academy of Sciences Dinner.......................................161
30. Inauguration of the Workers' College.................................168
31. Message to U Thant...169
32. Laying of the Foundation Stone at the Pre-fabricated Concrete Panel Factory...175
33. Christmas Message..178
34. New Year's Message...180

13TH ANNIVERSARY OF THE DECLARATION OF POSITIVE ACTION

January 8, 1963

Today is the 13th Anniversary of the day on which we declared Positive Action. Positive Action was the means by which we exerted political pressure for the achievement of our independence. As we celebrate this eventful day in our history, I come to salute you, the fighting members of our revolutionary Party.

Today Party branches throughout the country are celebrating this anniversary in a spirit of revival. Once again we are embarking upon Positive Action—positive action in reanimating that spirit of dynamism and solidarity that guided us through the successive phases of our struggle for national independence and unity.

Wherever we may be today, let all of us Ghanaians reflect upon the vital sequence of events that flowed from our adoption of Positive Action, both for Ghana and for Africa.

As you reflect, you will realise that it was your deep sense of discipline and comradeship that crowned our efforts in victory, and brought us to the proud and enviable position which we now hold. And you will not fail to draw inspiration from this dynamic period of our history and rededicate yourselves to the heavy tasks ahead.

The struggle for independence was not easy. Still we stood firm, secure in our unity of purpose and determination, which spurred our courage and patriotism and brought us victory in the battle for independence. After this battle was won, with the organised forces led by our Party, we were able within a short time to plan our first national programme, the fruit of our Party's identification with the well-being of the chiefs and people of Ghana.

We used our victory also to assist the struggle of our brothers for freedom in other parts of Africa. Comrades, the African revolution is the greatest political phenomenon of this latter half of the 20th century, and we of our great Party and of Ghana, should be proud that we are taking an active part in the revolution.

The struggle for the liberation and unity of Africa is paramount. The freedom and independence of every state and every territory in Africa is bound up with, and can only be realised in, the total emancipation of the African continent from political and economic imperialism. Without the political unity of Africa, the individual efforts of the several African states will be in vain, and the African masses will be the sufferers.

That is why, Comrades, I demand of every one of you the greatest effort and utmost devotion towards the realisation of our plans and objectives. Every one of you must rekindle that divine spark that flamed within our Party in the early stages of our struggle. For that is the spark that will re-animate our Party's dynamism and your devotion to our Party's purpose and its fulfilment.

On this 13th Anniversary of our historic Positive Action I expect every one of you to put aside selfish concerns, and in the spirit of comradeship and enthusiasm which characterised the Party during the first phase of our revolution, to stand shoulder to shoulder to bring to a successful conclusion the second phase of our revolution –the construction of a Socialist Ghana and a free and united Africa. Only the same dynamism and sense of unity which enable us to dislodge the forces of colonialism in Ghana can spur us on apace to this greater victory.

You must take seriously the diffusion of Party education. For it is through Party education that we will raise the political imperialist and neo-colonialist intrigues. It is only though Party education that we can secure the appreciation of the masses for our objective and engage their politically conscious support in achieving our aim of socialist transformation.

We must also re-dedicate ourselves anew to the service of Africa. We have completely defeated imperialism and colonialism in Ghana. We shall never allow them to raise their ugly heads again in this dear land of ours. Our enemies and detractors have tried unsuccessfully to arrest our progress, but you have demonstrated a solidarity and a loyalty that has frustrated and destroyed their hopes and plans. What remains for us to do now, is to advance into the ramparts of colonialism and imperialism in every part of Africa —wherever they may be—and to destroy them.

Comrades, you must re-arm yourselves in understanding and dedication for the task ahead. You must bury past inaction and bestir yourselves to give unselfishly of your best and utmost in helping to build Ghana into a prosperous and happy country, and in bringing independence and unity throughout Africa.

For we are determined to create a society in which no man shall fear oppression; a society in which all shall be free within the law: in which there shall be work for all and in which the condition for the happiness of each is the condition for the happiness of all; a socialist society that will be a blessing to all living within it.

And to succeed—as succeed we must, for the sake of the masses, whose interests are our prime concern and whose welfare is our supreme law—you must each devote yourselves without stint of thought of self to this sacred cause of Ghana's and Africa's redemption.

  Forward with the Party!

  Forward to African Unity!

  Forward to Socialism!

OFFICIAL OPENING OF KWAME NKRUMAH MARKET
Kumasi
February 16, 1963

I am sorry that I am unable to be with you on this joyful occasion of the official opening of the Kwame Nkrumah Market.

2. The amenities provided in this fine market will, I know, benefit greatly the people of Kumasi—sellers and buyers alike—and contribute to the economic development of this city. The construction of this market is another example of the positive and imaginative manner in which the Chairman and Councillors of the Kumasi City Council are discharging their duties towards the people of Kumasi, and their determination to provide you with all the modern amenities which are essential for your happiness and well-being.

3. I take this opportunity, therefore to convey to all those connected with the building of the market my warm congratulations for their enthusiastic and untiring efforts to introduce improvements in the city of Kumasi, and to build it into a veritable Garden City.

4. The Government is always ready to encourage and to assist local initiative and progressive ideas. I have recently directed that repayment of the loans granted by the Government to the Kumasi City Council and which the Council have spent for non-revenue earning projects in the interests of the Kumasi people should be waived. Furthermore, no interest will be charged on the remaining loans which have been used for commercial undertakings. These concessions will enable the Kumasi City Council to do more than it has done already for the people of this city

5. Municipal and Local Authorities, because their work impinges so directly on the lives of the people they serve, have a significant part to play in community development, and in our struggle to eliminate poverty, disease and illiteracy from Ghana and to raise the living standards of our people. You have a great opportunity to

assist in turning our cities, towns and villages into well planned and pleasant areas of habitation.

6. Let all Chairmen and Councillors of City, Municipal and Local Councils, Village and Town Committees rededicate themselves to their new responsibilities, and always remember their obligations to serve loyally and keep faith with the Party, the Government and the people.

3

DINNER WITH BUSINESSMEN

Flagstaff House
February 22, 1963

I am happy to welcome you here this evening. They say, I believe, that if you have something important to say, don't risk losing it in the digestive tracts of a hungry man. Now that you seem to me to be carefree and relaxed and in a mood of conviviality, "you'll have no scandal while we dine, but honest talk and wholesome wine."

Gentlemen: you are the representatives of industry and commerce, and constitute a vital part in the economic life of Ghana. I would like to take advantage of your presence here tonight to have a good look at our common problems.

As you know, we have had some problems in our foreign trade and balance of payments. The unsatisfactory state of world markets for cocoa and for some of our other major products made it necessary for us to tighten our belts. For those of you in the business community, your contribution to this effort has consisted mostly of having to keep within regulated limits the amounts which you could transfer abroad or pay out in dividends. In addition, we look steps to reduce our imports on goods in order to prevent the balance of payment crisis. We know that the reduction in imports has in some way affected your business, but I can assure you that the decision was taken in the interest of the nation, and especially of the national economy of which you form a part.

We know at the time that the measures we took would impose some restriction on all of us. Even those of us in the Government have felt the stress and strain of the limitations which the world financial situation imposed on our activities, but in spite of this, we must recognise the fact that these limitations were necessary in order to protect the strength and stability of our economy.

I am happy to say that as a result of the sacrifices made by the people of Ghana, by the Government and by you, the members of the business community, the financial situation has now stabilised. There has been a radical improvement in our balance of international trade, and the country's reserves have shown a healthy recovery. But this does not mean that the time has come for us to relax. Our economic position needs to be still further improved, particularly in the new period of development which we are about to enter with our Seven-Year Plan.

In the past year or so, while we have adopted these vigorous measures to protect Ghana's economy we have had to experiment with a number of devices in order to achieve our aim. I am fully aware of the difficulties which some of us have encountered owing to the changes that have to be made from time to time. I would like to say, however, that the Government of Ghana stands by the principles which I enumerated at the last Budget with regard to invest- ment, auld which I repeat here:

"The Government will continue to encourage private investors to establish and operate in Ghana.

"Our Government has no plans whatsoever to take over industries in the private sector; it is neither its wish to do so nor its aim or policy. When private investors enter into fields where state enterprises operate, they will compete on absolutely equal terms without discrimination."

Gentlemen, we must be frank and honest about our intentions and motives. There should be no secret doubts in the relations between us. We can only co-exist on the basis of absolute frankness. We, on our part, welcome every honest investor who wants to work for his equitable profits, but we shall not tolerate anyone who seeks to direct what political course we should follow. Any Government, or, for that matter, any organisation which invests in, or gives a loan or assistance to, another country like our own must on no account interfere directly or indirectly in the internal or external affairs of that country. If any attempt is made on the strength of such credit, loan, aid or assistance to interfere in the political, social, economic, cultural and military affairs of our country, then we shall consider that the motives under lying such activities and operations have a neo-colonialist character.

Perhaps between the theory and practice, there may have been some mistakes made in the application of the rules and regulations. I wish to say, therefore, that if any such mistakes have been made they have been made in good faith and with the best of intentions.

In order that such mistakes may not be repeated, I have instructed that the rules and regulations should now be put on a firm and clear-cut basis. You all know what is required of you, and I am confident that you will accept these in fairness and good spirit, and thereby contribute to the economic growth of Ghana. I am happy to say that an Investment Bill is nearing completion and is expected to be introduced shortly into Parliament. This Bill, when it becomes law, will provide legal backing to Government's policy with regard to investment and also, at the same time, define the nature of concessions which the Government proposes to make to investors.

Gentlemen, perhaps it will be a good thing for me at this juncture to say something about our hopes for the future.

We are in the process of establishing a society in which men and women will have no anxiety about work, food and shelter; where poverty and illiteracy no longer exist and where disease is brought under control; where our educational facilities provide our children with the best possible opportunities for learning; where every person uses his talents to their fullest capacity and contributes to the general well-being of the nation.

In order to attain these objectives, we have accepted the socialist pattern of society believing that at a certain level of economic growth of a less-developed country such as Ghana, State enterprise can co-exist with private business interests, provided certain rules are observed on both sides.

I have stated elsewhere that:

"There are circumstances in which the import of foreign capital is of benefit to the importing country, especially in the case of the emerging developing country where large-scale sources of capital accumulation is small and not so easy to mobilise. Foreign capital is thus useful and helpful if it takes the form of a loan or a credit to enable the borrowing country to buy what it needs from whatever sources it likes, and at the same time to retain the control of the assets to be developed.

"One of the worst things that can happen to less-developed and emerging countries is to receive foreign aid with political and economic strings attached. These aids are very often wrapped up in financial terms that are not easily discernible.

"Foreign investment made in an emerging and developing country by a foreign company in order that such company can make a profit, has nothing to do with aid. This does not mean that a developing country may not find it advantageous to make a contract with a foreign company for the setting up of, say, a factory or an industry.

"Real aid is something quite different. It consists of direct gifts or loan that are given on favourable terms and without strings attached.

"The problem therefore is how to obtain capital investment and still keep under sufficient control to prevent undue exploitation and how to preserve integrity and sovereignty without crippling economic or political ties to any country, block or system. In other words, can state enterprise and private enterprise co-exist in a less-developed country? I say yes, *provided they both conform to the general framework of the overall plan made by the State."*

As I have said earlier, our ideas of socialism can co-exist with private enterprise. I also believe that private capital and private investment capital, in particular, has a recognised and legitimate part to play in Ghana's economic development. We are consistent in these ideas. I have never made any secrets of my faith in socialist principles, but I have always tried to make it quite clear that Ghana's socialism is not incompatible with the existence and growth of a vigorous private sector in the economy.

Gentlemen, I need hardly say that Ghana expects you—indeed, Ghana invites you—businessmen, industrialists, bankers, manufacturers and investors, to play a significant role in this economic growth and development.

Let me end by saying—and I say this with emphasis and sincerity—that those of you who will be investing in Ghana will be investing in a very stable country: a country united; a country determined to make progress; a country determined to industrialise; a country determined to mechanise and diversify its agriculture; a country dynamic and honest in its intentions and consistent in its policies.

Look around the country for yourselves. Invite your business friends to come here and see with their own eyes the happy atmosphere pervading everything we do; the stability we rightly boast of; the buoyancy of our economy and the happy relationships existing between all races who live here. There can be no better assurance to investors than these. Tell them not to be taken in by the mischief of a section of the press in Europe and America.

And now, Gentlemen, let us stand and drink a toast to the progress and prosperity of trade and industry in Ghana.

UNIVERSITY DINNER
Flagstaff House
Accra
February 24, 1963

I am sorry that I was unable to be with you at the Convocation ceremony yesterday, but I am glad to welcome you here tonight.

I am pleased to see among us the students who graduated yesterday, and I would like to take this opportunity to express to them my best wishes for success in the years ahead of them. I hope that the knowledge they have gained in the University will stand them in good stead.

I would also like to congratulate most sincerely, Sir Arku Korsah, Mr. K. G. Konuah and Dr. Du Bois, who are the first to receive honorary degrees from the University of Ghana. We accept them warmly as alumni of Legon.

You who are with me tonight are connected in one way or another with the University of Ghana, and I know that you believe in the ideals for which a university institution like ours stands, namely, the pursuit of knowledge and the formation of character.

It is important also that there should be no doubt whatsoever in our minds as to what is the role of a university in a developing country such as Ghana.

The role of a university in a country like ours is to become the academic focus of national life, reflecting the social, economic, cultural and political aspirations of the people. It must kindle national interest in the youth and uplift our citizens and free them from ignorance, superstition and may I add, indolence. A university does not exist in a vacuum or in outer space. It exists in the context of a society, and it is there that it has its proper place. A university is supported by society, and without the sustenance which it receives from society, it will cease to exist.

We know that the objectives of a university cannot be achieved without scrupulous respect for academic freedom, for without academic freedom there can be no university. Teachers must be free to teach their subjects without any other concern than to convey to their students the truth as faithfully as they know it. Scholars must be free to pursue the truth and to publish the results of their researches without fear, for true scholarship fears nothing. It can even challenge the dead learning which has come to us from the cloistral and monastic schools of the middle ages. We know that without respect for academic freedom, in this sense, there can be no higher education worthy of the name, and, therefore, no intellectual progress, no flowering of the nation's mind. The genius of the people is stultified. We therefore cherish and shall continue to cherish academic freedom at our universities.

Speaking for myself, if I may do so with your permission, there was not an academic year in all my twelve years abroad when I was not at one university or another. I even augmented this with summer courses. I know the inside and outside of a university and I know the value of academic freedom. And I think you know what I am talking about.

Apart from the State, the university is one of the greatest institutions of man. The work of a university requires objectivity and honesty at every level. With malice to none, it is inspired only by a passionate concern for truth. It is therefore the business of the university to seek and to maintain that honesty and objectivity which are the only keys to progress.

Not only as Chancellor of the University, but also as President of Ghana, I would like to assure you of my readiness to defend at all times this right of the university, and to encourage all those who work within it—students, research scholars and professors—to work with honesty and objectivity.

There is, however, sometimes a tendency to use the words "academic freedom" in another sense, and to assert the claim that a university is more or less an institution of learning having no respect or allegiance to the community or to the country in which it exists and purports to serve. This assertion is unsound in principle and objectionable in practice. The university has a clear duty to the community which maintains it and which has the right to express concern for its pressing needs.

We know that academic freedom can be perverted and ever abused. It can also become a dangerous cloak for activities outside the academic interests and preoccupations of the community or of the university. Where this has happened a grave disservice is done to everything for which knowledge and truth really stand. True academic freedom—the intellectual freedom of the university—is everywhere fully compatible with service to the community; for the university is, and must always remain, a living, thinking and serving part of the community to which it belongs.

Let us be clear that it is not always from the outside that academic freedom can be threatened. University staff and the students themselves have a grave responsibility in maintaining this freedom, since they themselves can also be a threat to academic freedom of the university. They must always be ready to expose those individuals in the university itself who abuse academic freedom.

When I accepted the office of Chancellor, I promised you that I would do everything in my power to assist in promoting the successful development and prosperity of the University. I would like to take this opportunity to repeat this promise, legitimate endeavours in the interests of the University and the people of Ghana.

Everything I have said this evening has been prompted solely by my anxiety to ensure the success of our University, which is the pride of Ghana and many lands far beyond this country. The people of Ghana rightly expect that the University, in the words of the University Commission, should be fully responsive to the sense of urgency which animates them; to use its resources imaginatively and effectively to contribute to the economy of Ghana and of Africa, and to apply your studies for their benefit and to learn from their problems.

It should be the honour and responsibility of those of us who have had the privilege of the best education our country can afford to strive in every way possible to make our generation better than we found it. We must not only feel the pulse and intensity of the great African revolution taking place in our time, but we must also make a contribution of its realisation, progress and development.

Revolutionary Africa is a land of vigorous millions of people endowed with youthful energy and blessed with a sensitive humanism incompatible with the growth and maintenance of a privileged class. You who pass through the portable of our universities should be constantly aware of your oneness with the people and your responsibility towards them. This is our challenge and opportunity, and all of us—professors, teachers, alumni and students alike—must strive to maintain this great heritage which has been handed to us.

And let us nourish this heritage and pass it on to the next generation unalloyed and untarnished.

And now, I ask you all to rise and drink with me a toast—a toast to the progress and development of University education in Ghana.

5

ON THE EVE OF
6TH INDEPENDENCE ANNIVERSARY

Accra
March 5, 1963

Tomorrow is the Sixth Anniversary of the attainment of our independence. As yon know, you will observe This day as a public holiday.

Normally the 6th of March is marked by public celebrations throughout the country. During the past year, however, we have been engaged in checking criminal and anti-social activities by a few people among us, instigated by outside influences, which have resulted in death and injury to some of our countrymen and women. For this reason, and for the sake of those who have been the unfortunate victims of these crimes, no public ceremonies will be held tomorrow.

It is my hope that while you enjoy the holiday, you will remember those among us who are suffering for the wicked activities of a selfish few; and that whatever the form of your enjoyment tomorrow, you will spend a little time in quiet meditation about the safety and security of our nation.

I have directed that next Sunday, the 10th of March, should be observed by all churches in Ghana as a day of prayer for the nation. The trial of those persons who have been involved in these acts of terrorism and murder against their fellow citizens will begin next Friday, the 8th of March.

Countrymen, ours is a society in which men and women have always been free to go about their legitimate business without fear or danger to life and limb. It is our duty and privilege to maintain this enviable record. Our aim is to ensure that by our united efforts, every man and woman in Ghana will have the right to work and enjoy the fruits of his labour and to live a decent and honest life. Our doors are open to all who are willing and ready to help us build our new society. All those who help us in this way, no matter where they come from, are welcome as our friends. But those who seek to defraud and exploit us and the state, or consort with wicked men, subversive elements and agencies, cannot honestly regard themselves as friends of Ghana.

Let us not under-estimate the resourcefulness of our detractors and those who for one reason or another do not wish us well. Whenever and wherever we meet any of their agents, we should not fail to bring home to them the grave risks they run by acting as stooges, quislings and traitors against the interest of the nation.

Steadily and consistently we are building up a better and richer life for our people and our country. We are developing a society free from racial discrimination, a society in which people of different continents and different religious sects and beliefs, can work together without molestation, a society in which the relation between man and man is fundamentally based on the social process of production. If we continue to maintain this harmony and work together for the common good, the plans which the Government has already set in motion for our progress, happiness and development, will bear rich fruit for us all.

I wish you all happiness and joy in your holiday.

Good luck and good night.

6
SIXTH INDEPENDENCE ANNIVERSARY DIPLOMATIC DINNER

State House
Accra
March 6, 1963

The Dean of the Diplomatic Corps has warned me that in speaking to you this evening, I will be talking to "professional analysts," which means, I fear, that every word I utter will be carefully examined, dissected and weighed. While you busy yourselves so, please remember one thing: you are diplomats and I am not! I sometimes wonder what category I do come under these days. I wonder, for instance, if I am even a politician? Since, however, I am what I am, I intend to say what little I have to say tonight, freely and without diplomatic delicacy!

As we look at the world today, we cannot pretend to be optimistic that the problems of peace and war, colonialism and disarmament are nearer solution than before. In spite of the limited successes achieved in the attempts to solve these problems, they still constitute the most glaring paradox of our modern age.

I know, however, that you who are members of the diplomatic corps, are as dedicated as we are to the preservation of peace, the abolition of war, the liquidation of colonialism and the achievement of general and complete disarmament.

As I have said elsewhere, the balance of forces in the world today has reached such a stage that the only avenue open to mankind is co-existence. The only alternative to this is chaos, destruction and perhaps even complete annihilation. As I see it, mankind must decide whether it prefers the "world without the bomb" or "the bomb without the world."

It is because of our ardent desire in Ghana for the achievement of world peace that we took steps last year to sponsor the Accra Assembly on the World Without the Bomb. Without world peace neither Ghana nor, indeed, the rest of the African Continent can hope to maintain a steady rate of progress and development.

In the wider field of international life, development is seriously hampered by the conflicts which break out between the great power blocks. We cannot, however, speak of a balance of forces, or even of co-existence or peace itself, so long as any vestiges of colonialism remain anywhere in the world.

Ghana's foreign policy has been clearly stated on many occasions. Our policy in Africa is to support by all legitimate means those countries still struggling for their liberation from the colonial yoke. We also believe that the true voice of Africa can only emerge from a political Union of the Independent African States.

Such a Union will enable the Continent to exploit and develop its resources to the fullest capacity for the benefit of the states which shall compose it.

Externally, we seek co-operation and friendship with all nations, based on a policy of positive neutralism and non-alignment.

Ghana's African policy and our policy of positive neutralism and non-alignment have often been deliberately misinterpreted, but I believe that our stand has made it possible for us to preserve our moral stature and has also enabled us to keep a balanced view on international issues.

In the past Africa was the scene of slavery, colonial exploitation and oppressive rule. Today there is a new Africa and a new African; an African who refuses to succumb to the blandishments of the imperialists, colonialists and neo-colonialists and rejects any policies inimical to the interest of the peoples of Africa. This new Africa is ready to fulfil its destiny and play its part in the establishment of the grand and peaceful new world order to which mankind is dedicated.

It is in this spirit that I wish to assure you, representatives of your governments in Ghana, of my deep appreciation for the spirit of co-operation and understanding which has characterised the relations between us. We have had our differences, our diplomatic ups and downs and our clashes. But what are you here in Ghana for, anyway?

Ladies and Gentlemen, I am reminded here of a traditional Ananse story which I would like to tell you. Ananse bought a large piece of virgin forest for cultivation. The day came when he wanted to clear this land and, as is the custom, he invited all his friends of the forest to come and help him. They came willingly; the snake and the toad, the farmer and his cutlass, the hen and the hawk, the cat and the mouse, the lion and the deer and the elephant. Fire and water came along too, one to burn the twigs, the other to refresh the labourers. They gathered there for one purpose; to help Ananse clear his land.

But Ananse was a mischief-maker. As soon as he gave the order to start work, he hid behind a tree to enjoy the spectacle which he had planned. First the farmer chased the snake and battered him to death with his cutlass. Then the hawk swooped down and attacked the hens. The cat caught and ate the mouse, the lion the deer and the elephant trumpeted about killing with his heavy feet those animals who were still alive. The fire and water were both lost in a heavy downpour of rain.

Because of Ananse's destructive deed, all was lost.

Ladies and Gentlemen; there, but for the grace of sweet reasonableness, goes mankind; Let us learn to live and let live while there is yet time. If we are to work together for the peace and happiness of mankind, we must learn to do better than Ananse and his animal friends.

And now, may I ask you to drink with me a toast—a toast to friendship and co-operation among nations.

7

VOLTA RIVER PROJECT
TO THE NATIONAL ASSEMBLY

Accra
March 25, 1963

Mr. Speaker; Members of the National Assembly: on February 21st, 1961, I made a comprehensive statement to the Assembly about the Volta River Project. In my subsequent statements in January and September, 1962, I indicated briefly the progress which had then been made in the work on the Project. I propose to tell you today of what I saw at the Dam site at Akosombo during my inspection visit on February 19th this year and to convey to you the sense of thrill and joy, and the hopes and aspirations, which revived in my mind at the sight of the translation of the cherished dream of a generation into masses of rock-fill, slush grout and concrete in different, phases of the Project.

You may recall that I participated in the ground-breaking ceremony at Akosombo just about a year ago. These past twelve months have seen steady progress of work in all activities according to the schedule of the Contractors, Impregilo and Company. It is an exhilarating experience to the see the transformation of the whole scene at Akosombo. The surging, rushing waters of the great Volta River have now been tamed by the upstream and downstream coffer-dams, and in future, the bulk of water will flow downstream through the 1,000 feet long Diversion Tunnel. Our Engineers were baffled for a time, with the de-watering of the area between the two coffer-dams but they have overcome the problem, and there is every expectation that the construction work will proceed smoothly in the coming months.

Twenty-five per cent of the construction of the dam has already been completed, and all phases of the project are on schedule. The Consulting Engineers, the principal Contractors and all Ghanaian nationals and expatriate staff engaged in this great work deserve our warm commendation.

The immediate objective now in the construction programme of the main dam will be to build the dam as high as possible above the rock foundation of the river bottom prior to the start of this year's flood season. The programme will be interrupted to allow the flood waters to flow over the uncompleted dam. After the flood subsides the construction of the dam is scheduled to rise to such a height that when the floods of 1964 arrive they will be impounded above the dam, and Lake Volta will start to form.

A monumental task to be completed before the formation of the lake is the resettlement of about 70,000 people from the inundated area. It is the policy of this Government that no one should be worse off as a result of the Volta River Project. The movement of the people involved is therefore being planned to provide them with new villages with better communal facilities and better farming methods. This activity which is being co-ordinated by the Volta River Authority relies on the support of all governmental agencies and Ministries as well as the full co-operation and the efforts of the people themselves.

The Volta River Project and its ancillary activities represent the largest single investment in the development plan of our country. It is important, therefore, that every one in Ghana should fully understand how the project is being financed and the sacrifices which we are making for its realisation.

The project itself, comprising the dam, the power house and the transmission lines, envisages a total capital outlay of some G70 million pounds. One half of the amount, that is G35 million pounds, is being provided by the Government of Ghana, in other words, by the people of Ghana. In order to meet the remaining G35 million pounds, we have accepted loans at commercial interest from the World Bank, the two United States Government's Agencies, namely, the Export and Import Bank and Agency for International Development, and from the Export Credits Guarantee Department of the Government of the United Kingdom. Let us be quite clear that these loans which are being provided from abroad are not free grants or gifts. They are commercial loans which will have to be repaid by us at rates of interest ranging from $3^1/_2$ percent to $5^3/_4$ per cent. So far, we have drawn very little against these loans.

The preliminary site works at Akosombo, which we built in 1959 ahead of schedule and in advance of the signing of the various agreements, cost us some G2 million pounds. This early action on our part has had the effect of reducing by one full year the time required to construct the project. We must also remember that Tema Harbour and Tema Township, which represent an integral part of the Volta River Project, have been constructed from our own resources at a cost of nearly £G30 million pounds.

Furthermore, we have matched our faith and belief in this project by bearing the brunt of the expenditure in respect of the project in the initial years. The total expenditure over the project from its inception to the end of February, 1963 is estimated about G3 million pounds. Over 90 per cent of this amount has been paid by the Government of Ghana as part of its 50 percent share of the capital outlay.

The Volta Project will confer numerous direct benefits on the national economy. It will create larger avenues of gainful employment to Ghanaian nationals both in the construction and final operational stages. Currently, about 3,000 Ghanaians are working at Akosombo and taking advantage of the opportunity of learning technical skills on the job. The Power House, the Transmission System and the Smelter may provide new jobs for over 2,000 skilled and semi-skilled workers. The abundant supply of electrical power will bring light to thousands of homes in the countryside where darkness now prevails. It will make available power practically at the door-steps of business men and entrepreneurs in urban areas and offer them a powerful stimulus for the modernisation of existing industries and the development of new ones. The increased use of electricity will help to reduce the foreign exchange expenditure on imported fuel oil. The production of aluminium ingots will add to the range of Ghana's export and stimulate a greater development of our rich bauxite resources.

While the Volta River Project has been conceived mainly as a hydro-electric project, the Government is not unmindful of its vast potential for development in several other sectors of our economy. The vast artificial lake extending over 300 miles with a surface area of 3,275 square miles may provide practical possibilities for developing a system of inland navigation and transportation through a network of harbours on the lake. This will help to open up the inland areas and encourage larger movements of agricultural produce, forest products and fruits from those areas to be principal consuming markets. The development of inland fisheries in suitable areas of the lake also offers another possibility. With these facts in mind, the Government have already employed a competent group of Consulting Engineers to advise on the prospects of lake transportation system. The development of fisheries is also engaging attention. On the one hand, the Volta River Project may have to be mainly a hydro-electric project as the bulk of the useful storage water in the reservoir behind the Dam will be needed to produce electric power. On the other hand, the regulated downstream flow of water below the Dam may offer real possibilities for scientific irrigated agriculture comprising heavy water-using crops such as sugar-cane, rice and irrigated cotton. These possibilities will soon be investigated by competent technicians.

As the construction work at Akosombo proceeds steadily according to schedule, the promise and the prospect which the combined Volta and VALCO Project offers for Ghana's economic growth and development begin to get into focus and stand out in their proper perspective. The Volta River Project is both a challenge and an opportunity; a challenge because it calls for dedication, public spirit and hard work from the personnel engaged on the work as well as the leaders of public opinion and the people at large; an opportunity because it calls for a high degree of resourcefulness and initiative on the part of farmers, workers and entrepreneurs in Ghana.

I would like to urge the Members of the National Assembly to visit the Dam site at Akosombo from time to time and to persuade their constituents and friends here and abroad to come and see this gigantic dream come true. It is indeed an inspiring experience to visit the Dam site and imbibe the message of hope and growth it conveys for our Nation. Major projects such as the Volta are the new "places of Pilgrimage" in this modern Age of Science and Technology. They serve as monuments to the determination and dedication of a whole people to raise themselves to a fuller and richer life. In this noble endeavour, we welcome foreign Capital—institutional or Private—from all sources, provided it is offered without strings and it is attracted to this country not merely by the economic viability of projects but especially by a spirit of true partnership and a willingness to help to build up Ghana's prosperity and the welfare of its people on enduring foundations.

8
WORLD YOUTH DAY

Flagstaff House
Accra
April 23, 1963

On the occasion of World Youth Day, I am happy to send this message to the youth of Ghana.

We are passing through an important and exciting phase not only in the reconstruction and development of our country, but also in the struggle for the freedom and unity of our great continent. In this great task of reconstruction all of you have vital part to play. In this spirit, I ask you to rededicate yourselves, in loyalty and patriotism, for the service of your country and Africa.

If we are to succeed in our endeavours the youth of today must cultivate the virtues which we expect of Africa's new man. Our youth must be strong, of good character; of great moral courage, humble, hardworking, polite, responsible, reliable and scrupulously honest. These are the virtues on which we can build Ghana and make it a prosperous and happy place to live in.

Go forward and march together, in unity and strength, as one family and one people.

In all things, remember that our great Party—the Convention People's Party—stand behind you as the bulwark of your assumptions.

9

MAY DAY BROADCAST

Accra
April 30, 1963

Tomorrow is May Day, a day on which Socialists and the working class movements all over the world re-dedicate themselves to the ideals of work and happiness for the people. On this occasion it is fitting that we in Ghana should renew our determination to build our country in such a way as to create opportunity for work for all.

It is fitting that we should reflect, at this time, on the national goals we have set before us and examine whether the conditions we are providing in our society are such as to enable our men and women, particularly our youth, to play their full part in this task of national reconstruction.

This is why I want to speak to you tonight, particularly about some of the things we can do to help our young men and women to make full use of the opportunities available to them, and thus prepare themselves for the future.

In a few months from now, we shall launch our Seven-Year Development Plan, which is intended to transfer Ghana into a modern, industrial state. But even now it is admitted by those who visit us that our progress has been remarkable and impressive. Look around you, and see our new factories, hospitals, schools and Universities springing up all over the country. There is hardly a remote village which has not benefited already from the great strides made in our progress and development.

But what is all this advancement for, if we do not support and sustain it with a strong moral and spiritual foundation. If we combine moral degeneration with technological and scientific progress, then Ghana will surely fail. This of course has been the lesson of history. Look at the temperament, attitude towards work, honesty and integrity of the men and women of any people, and you have a good indication how low or how high is the moral and spiritual quality of the nation.

Many foreigners who come to Ghana are genuinely impressed by the obvious signs of progress they see around them. They also admire the cheerful spirit and enthusiasm of the men and women in the streets. This leads them to expect a high standard of efficiency, hard work, responsibility and energy from us whether in the offices, work-places, factories, farms, building sites, shops and public counters, in the streets, lorry parks and taxi ranks. But what do they find?

Their first experience on the telephone disillusions them. Some of our telephone girls who are normally so friendly, polite and well-behaved at home, are often rude and abrupt when dealing with subscribers.

In the shops, the assistants ignore customers while they chat among themselves and treat them with nonchalance and disrespect, forgetting that but for these same customers they would not be in employment.

The conditions are no better in the public services. Those who go to the Post Offices to buy stamps, postal orders or take delivery of parcels know this so well.

Look at our hospitals where the very lives of the people who may be our own fathers and mothers, or husbands and wives, or brothers and sisters may depend on the care and attention they receive. Even here, you will sometimes find such inhuman disregard for pain and suffering as to make you shake your head in shame.

Look at the laziness and insolent attitude of many of our boys and girls or our young men and women at work and in the public places. Surely, with all the opportunities provided by the State for, them, our young people should be more vigorous and responsible than this.

I am appalled at the reports that reach me about the behaviours of our young women in the bars, dance halls, and other public places. These young women will be the mothers of the next generation, and they have a duty to themselves and to Ghana to maintain the highest standard of health, decency and morality in our society.

Countrymen, this sort of attitude to life and work is not only anti-social, it is criminal, it cuts at the very roots of our national life.

We must emulate the example of the many devoted and dedicated men and women among us to whom work is more than merely to earn a living.

I have also been greatly concerned about the falling standards of courtesy and politeness among our youth. These days we seldom hear the words "thank you" or "meda wo ase." We take kindness and goodwill for granted. We no longer say "Yes Sir" or "No Sir" to our elders.

Countrymen, we must all work to revive those virtues and values in our society on which our fathers based their high standards of moral conduct and behaviour.

The Young Pioneer Movement is already doing a great work in inculcating in the youth of Ghana a true spirit of humility, of service and of devotion to the country.

Plans are ready for establishing very soon, a Gliding School at Afienya, which I hope will attract many of our youth. The training will give them a sense of self-reliance, and adventure which will be of great use to them in their life and work.

In order to help inculcate more deeply these ideals in our youth and to ensure that our youth grow up upright and respect all the good things which make life worthwhile, I have directed that every morning the Ghana flag should be raised at all schools at the morning parades, and that the pupils say this national pledge with raised hands:

> "I promise on my honour to be faithful to Ghana,
> To serve her with all my strength and with all my heart;
> And in all things to uphold Ghana's good name. So help me God."

The Government has also decided to introduce as soon as possible a system of national training. This training will be so arranged that immediately prior to admission to Secondary Schools, all male children will do a three-month period of national training. At the end of secondary school course and prior to attendance at a University they will undergo a further three-month training; furthermore, all University graduates on leaving the University will do six months training before taking their places in life of our society.

The purpose of this scheme is to inculcate in our young people and our youth the virtues and disciplines such as the spirit of service, love for work, a sense of responsibility and dedication of devotion to Ghana and Africa, of respect for our elders and superiors, and of self-discipline and earnestness. I am of the firm opinion that this national service scheme, if fully auld properly implemented, will give our youth not only physical health but mental, spiritual and moral upliftment.

Let us remember that the eyes of the world are upon us in whatever we do. We have been able through our united effort to set the pace for the liberation and unity of our continent. We must therefore strive to uphold auld maintain the force and influence of the African revolution to which we are so deeply committed. We cannot do this unless we can produce young men and women with the highest ideals of work and service to the nation and to our great continent.

I hope that all existing organisations, especially the Churches, which have the moral welfare of our people at heart will, in their part in this national crusade for the moral and spiritual advancement of our people.

I wish you all a happy May Day celebration.

10

CONFERENCE OF AFRICAN HEADS OF STATE AND GOVERNMENT

Addis Ababa
May 24, 1963

I am happy to be here in Addis Ababa on this most historic occasion. I bring with me the hopes and fraternal greetings of the Government and people of Ghana to His Imperial Majesty Haille Selassie and to all Heads of African States gathered here in this ancient capital in this momentous period in our history. Our objective is African Union now. There is no time to waste. We must unite now or perish. I am confident that by our concerted effort and determination we shall lay here the foundations for a continental Union of African States.

At the first gathering of African Heads of State, to which I had the honour of playing host, there were representatives of eight independent State only. Today, five years later, here at Addis Ababa, we meet as the representatives of no less than thirty-two States, the guests of His Imperial Majesty, Haille Selassie the First, and the Government and people of Ethiopia. To His Imperial Majesty, I wish to express, on behalf of the Government and people of Ghana my deep appreciation of a most cordial welcome and generous hospitality.

The increase in our number in this short space of time is open testimony to the indomitable and irresistible surge of our peoples for independence. It is also a token of the revolutionary speed of world events in the latter half of this century. In the task which is before us of unifying our continent we must fall in with that pace or be left behind. The task cannot be attacked in the tempo of any other age than our own. To tall behind the unprecedented momentum of actions and events in our time will be to court failure and our own undoing.

A whole continent has imposed a mandate upon us to lay the

foundation of our Union at this Conference. It is our responsibility to execute this mandate by creating here and now the formula upon which the requisite superstructure may be erected.

On this continent it has not taken us long to discover that the struggle against colonialism does not end with the attainment of national independence. Independence is only the prelude to a new and more involved struggle for the right to conduct our own economic and social affairs, to construct our society according to our aspirations, unhampered by crushing and humiliating neo-colonialist controls and interference.

From the start we have been threatened with frustration where rapid change is imperative and with instability where sustained effort and ordered rule are indispensable.

No sporadic act nor pious resolution can resolve our present problems. Nothing will be of avail, except the united act of a united Africa. We have already reached the stage where we must unite or sink into that condition which has made Latin-America the unwilling and distressed prey of imperialism after one-and-a-half centuries of political independence.

As a continent we have emerged into independence in a different age, with imperialism grown stronger, more ruthless and experienced, and more dangerous in international associations. Our economic advancements demands the end of colonialist and neo-colonialist domination in Africa.

But just as we understood that the shaping of our national destinies required of each of us our political independence and bent all our strength to this attainment, so we must recognise that our economic independence resides in our African union and requires the same concentration upon the political achievement.

The unity of our continent, no less than our separate independence, will be delayed if, indeed, we do not lose it, by hobnobbing with colonialism. African Unity is, above all, a political kingdom which can only be gained by political means. The social and economic development of Africa will come only within the political kingdom, not the other way round. The United States of America, the Union of

Soviet Socialist Republics, were the political decisions of revolutionary peoples before they became mighty realities of social power and material wealth.

How, except by our united efforts, will the richest and still enslaved parts of our continent be freed from colonial occupation and become available to us for the total development of our continent? Every step in the decolonisation of our continent has brought greater resistance in those areas where colonial garrisons are available to colonialism and you all here know that.

This is the great design of the imperialist interests that buttress colonialism and neo-colonialism, and we would be deceiving ourselves in the most cruel way were we to regard their individual actions as separate and unrelated. When Portugal violates Senegal's border, when Verwoerd allocates one-seventh of South Africa's budget to military and police, when France builds as part of her defence policy an interventionist force that can intervene, more especially in French-speaking Africa, when Welensky talks of, Southern Rhodesia joining South Africa, when Britain sends arms to South Africa, it is all part of a carefully calculated pattern working towards a single end; the continued enslavement of our still dependent brothers and an onslaught upon the independence of our sovereign African states.

Do we have any other weapon against this design but our unity? Is not our unity essential to guard our own freedom as well as to win freedom for our oppressed brothers, the Freedom Fighters? Is it not unity alone that can weld us into an effective force, capable of creating our own progress and making our valuable contribution to world, peace? Which independent African State, which of you here will claim that its financial structure and banking institutions are fully harnessed to its national development? Which will claim that its material resources and human energies are available for its own national aspirations? Which will disclaim substantial measure of disappointment and disillusionment in its agricultural and urban development?

In independent Africa we are already re-experiencing the instability and frustration which existed under colonial rule. We are fast learning that political independence is not enough to rid us of the consequences of colonial rule.

The movement of the masses of the people of Africa for freedom, from that kind of rule was not only a revolt against the conditions which it imposed.

Our people supported us in our fight for independence because they believed that African Governments could cure the ills of the past in a way which could never be accomplished under colonial rule. If, therefore, now that we are independent we allow the same conditions to exist that existed in colonial days, all the resentment which overthrew colonialism will be mobilised against us.

The resources are there. It is for us to marshal them in the active service of our people. Unless we do this by our concerted efforts, within the framework of our combined planning, we shall not progress at the tempo demanded by today's events and the mood of our people. The symptoms of our troubles will grow, and the troubles themselves become chronic. It will then be too late even for Pan African Unity to secure for us stability and tranquillity in our labours for a continent of social justice and material well-being. Unless we establish African Unity now, we who are sitting here today shall tomorrow be the victims and martyrs of neo-colonialism.

There is evidence on every side that the imperialists have not withdrawn from our affairs. There are times, as in the Congo, when their interference is manifest. But generally it is covered up under the clothing of many agencies, which meddle in our domestic affairs, to torment dissension within our borders and to create an atmosphere of tension and political instability. As long as we do not do away with the root causes of discontent, we lend aid to these neo-colonialist forces, and shall become our own executioners. We can not ignore the teachings of history.

Our continent is probably the richest in the world for minerals and industrial and agricultural primary materials. From the Congo alone, Western firms exported copper, rubber, cotton, and other goods to the value of 2,773 million dollars in the ten years between 1945 and 1955, and from South Africa, Western gold mining companies have drawn a profit, in the six years between 1947 to 1951, of 814 million dollars.

Our continent certainly exceeds all the others in potential hydro-electric power, which some experts assess as 42 per cent of the world's total. What need is there for us to remain hewers of wood and drawers of water for the industrialised areas of the world?

It is said, of course, that we have no capital, no industrial skill, no communications and no internal markets, and that we cannot even agree among ourselves how best to utilise our resources for our own social needs.

Yet all the stock exchanges in the world are pre-occupied with Africa's gold, diamonds, uranium, platinum, copper and iron ore. Our capital flows out in streams to irrigate the whole system of Western economy. Fifty-two per cent of the gold in Fort Knox at this moment, where the U. S. A. stores its bullion, is believed to have originated from our shores. Africa provides more than 60 per cent of the world's gold. A great deal of the uranium for nuclear power, of copper for electronics, of titanium for supersonic projectiles, of iron and steel for heavy industries, of other minerals and raw materials for lighter industries—the basic economic might of the foreign Powers—come from our continent.

Experts have estimated that the Congo basin alone can produce enough food crops to satisfy the requirements of nearly half the population of the whole world and here we sit talking about regionalism, talking about gradualism, talking about step by step. Are you afraid to tackle the bull by the horn?

For centuries Africa has been the milk cow of the Western world. Was it not our continent that helped the Western world to build up its accumulated wealth?

It is true that we are now throwing off the yoke of colonialism as fast as we can, but our success in this direction is equally matched by an intense effort on the part of imperialism to continue the exploitation of our resources by creating divisions among us.

When the colonies of the American Continent sought to free

themselves from imperialism in the 18th century there was no threat of neo-colonialism in the sense on which we know it today in Africa. The American States were therefore free to form and fashion the unity which was best united to their needs and to frame constitution to hold their unity together without any form of interference from external sources. We, however, are having to grapple with outside interventions. How much more, then do we need to come together in the African unity that alone can save us from the clutches of neo-colonialism and imperialism.

We have the resources. It was colonialism in the first place that prevented us from accumulating the effective capital; but we ourselves have failed to make full use of our power in independence to mobilise our resources for the most effective take-off into thorough going economic and social development. We have been too busy nursing our separate states to understand fully the basic need of our union, rooted in common purpose, common planning and common endeavour. A union that ignores these fundamental necessities will be but a sham. It is only by uniting our productive capacity and the resultant production that we can amass capital. And once we start, the momentum will increase. With capital controlled by our own banks, harnessed to our own true industrial and agricultural development, we shall make our advance. We shall accumulate machinery and establish steel works, iron foundries and factories; we shall link the various states of our continent with communications by land, sea and air. We shall cable from one place to another, phone from one place to the other and astound the world with our hydro-electric power; we shall drain marshes and swamps, clear infested areas, feed the under-nourished, and rid our people of parasites and disease. It is within the possibility of science and technology to make even the Sahara bloom into a vast field with verdant vegetation for agricultural and industrial developments. We shall harness the radio, television, giant printing presses to lift our people from the dark recesses of illiteracy.

A decade ago, these would have been visionary words, the fantasies of an idle dreamer. But this is the age in which science has transcended the limits of the material world, and technology has invaded the silences of nature. Time and space have been reduced to unimportant abstractions. Giant machines make roads, clear forests, dig dams, lay out aerodromes; mounter trucks and planes distribute goods; huge laboratories manufacture drugs; complicated geological surveys are made; mighty power stations are built; colossal factories erected - all at an incredible speed. The world is no longer moving through bush paths or on camels and donkeys.

We cannot afford to pace our needs, our development, our security, to the gait of camels and donkeys. We cannot afford not to cut down the overgrown bush of outmoded attitudes that obstruct our path to the modem open road of the widest and earliest achievement of economic independence and the raising up of the lives of our people to the highest level.

Even for other continents lacking the resources of Africa, this is the age that sees the end of human want. For us it is a simple matter of grasping with certainty our heritage by using the political might of unity: All we need to do is to develop with our united strength the enormous resources of our continent. A United Africa will provide a stable field of foreign investment, which will be encouraged as soon as it does not behave inimically to our African interests. For such investment would add by its enterprises to the development of the continental national economy, employment and training of our people, and will be welcome Africa. In dealing with a united Africa, investors will no longer have to weigh with concern the risks of negotiating with governments in one period which may not exist in the very next period. Instead of dealing or negotiating with so many separate states at a time, they will be dealing with one united government pursuing a harmonised continental policy.

What is the alternative to this? If we falter at this stage, and let time pass for neo-colonialism to consolidate its position on this continent, what will be the fate of our people who have put their trust in us? What will be the fate of our freedom fighters? What will be the fate of other African territories that are not yet free?

Unless we can establish great industrial complexes in Africa—which we can only do in a united Africa—we must leave our peasantry to the mercy of foreign cash crop markets, and face the same unrest which overthrew the colonialists. What use to the farmer is education and mechanisation, what use is even capital for development, unless we can ensure for him a fair price and a ready market? What has the peasant, worker and farmer gained from political independence, unless we can ensure for him a fair return for his labour and higher standard of living?

Unless we can establish great industrial complexes in Africa, what have the urban worker, and those peasants on overcrowded land gained from political independence? If they are to remain unemployed or in unskilled occupation, what will avail them the better facilities for education, technical training, energy and ambition which independence enables us to provide?

There is hardly any African State without a frontier problem with, its adjacent neighbours. It would be futile for me to enumerate them because they are already so familiar to us all. But let me suggest to Your Excellencies that this fatal relic of colonialism will drive us to war against one another as our unplanned and uncoordinated industrial development expands, just as happened in Europe. Unless we succeed in arresting the danger through mutual understanding on fundamental issues and through African Unity, which will render existing boundaries obsolete and superfluous, we shall have fought in vain for independence. Only African Unity can heal this festering sore of boundary disputes between our various states. Your Excellencies, the remedy for these ills is ready in our hand. It stares us in the face at every customs barrier, it shouts to us from every African heart. By creating a true political union of all the independent states of Africa, with executive powers for political direction we can tackle hopefully every emergency, every enemy, and every complexity. This is not because we are a race of supermen, but because we have emerged in the age of science and technology in, which poverty, ignorance and disease are no longer the masters, but the retreating foes of mankind. We have emerged in the age of socialised planning, when production and distribution are not governed by chaos, greed and self-interest, but by social needs. Together with the rest of mankind, we have awakened from Utopian dreams to pursue practical blueprints for progress and social justice.

Above all, we have merged at a time when a continental land mass like Africa with its population approaching three hundred million are necessary to the economic capitalisation and profitability of modern productive methods and techniques. Not one of us working singly and individually can successfully attain the fullest development. Certainly, in the circumstances, it will not be possible to give adequate assistance to sister states trying, against the most difficult conditions, to improve their economic and social structures. Only a united Africa functioning under a Union Government can forcefully mobilise the material and moral resources of our separate countries and apply them efficiently and energetically to bring a rapid change in the conditions of our people.

If we do not approach the problems in Africa with a common front and a common purpose, we shall be haggling and wrangling among ourselves until we are colonised again and become the tools of a far greater colonialism than we suffered hitherto.

United we must. Without necessarily sacrificing our sovereignties, big or small, we can here and now forge a political union based on Defence, Foreign Affairs and Diplomacy, and a Common Citizenship, an African Currency, an African Monetary Zone and an African Central Bank. We must unite in order to achieve the full liberation of our continent. We need a Common Defence System with an African High Command to ensure the stability and security of Africa.

We have been charged with this sacred task by our own people, and we cannot betray their trust by failing them. We will be mocking the hopes of our people if we show the slightest hesitation or delay in tackling realistically this question of African Unity.

The supply of arms or other military aid to the colonial oppressors in Africa must be regarded not only as aid in the vanquishment of the freedom fighters battling for their African independence, but as an act of aggression against the whole of Africa. How can we meet this aggression except by the full weight of our united strength?

Many of us have made non-alignment an article of faith on this continent. We have no wish, and no intention of being drawn into the Cold War. But with the present weakness and insecurity of our States in the context of world politics, the search for bases and spheres of influence brings the Cold War into Africa with its danger of nuclear warfare. Africa should be declared a nuclear-free zone and freed from cold war exigencies. But we cannot make this demand mandatory unless we support it from a position of strength to be found only in our unity.

Instead, many Independent African States are involved in military pacts with the former colonial powers. The stability and security which such devices seek to establish are illusory, for the metropolitan Powers seize the opportunity to support their neo-colonialist controls by direct military involvement. We have seen how the neo-colonialists use their bases to entrench themselves and even to attack neighbouring independent states. Such bases are centres of tension and potential danger spots of military conflict. They threaten the security not only of the country in which they are situated but of neighbouring countries as well. How can we hope to make Africa a nuclear-free zone and independent of cold war pressure with such military involvement on our continent? Only by counter-balancing a common defence force with a common desire for an Africa untrammelled by foreign dictation or military and nuclear presence. This will require an all-embracing African High Command, especially if the military pacts with the imperialists are to be renounced. It is the only way we can break these direct links between the colonialism of the past and the neo-colonialism which disrupts us today.

We do not want nor do we visualise an African High Command in the terms of the power politics that now rule a great part of the world, but as an essential and indispensable instrument for ensuring stability and security in Africa.

We need a unified economic planning for Africa. Until the economic power of Africa is in our hands, the masses can have no real concern and no real interest for safeguarding our security, for ensuring the stability of our regimes, and for bending their strength to the fulfilment of our ends. With our united resources, energies and talents we have the means, as soon as we show the will, to transform the economic structures of our individual states from poverty to that of wealth, from inequality to the satisfaction of popular needs. Only on a continental basis shall we be able to plan the proper utilisation of all our resources for the full development of our continent.

How else will we retain our own capital for our development? How else will we establish an internal market for our own industries?

By belonging to different economic zones, how will we break down the currency and trading barriers between African States, and how will the economically stronger amongst us be able to assist the weaker and less developed States?

It is important to remember that independent financing and independent development cannot take place without an independent currency. A currency system that is backed by the resources of a foreign state is *ipso facto* subject to the trade and financial arrangements of that foreign country.

Because we have so many customs and currency barriers as a result of being subject to the different currency systems of foreign powers, this has served to widen the page between us in Africa. How, for example, can related communities and families trade with, and support one another successfully, if they find themselves divided by national boundaries and currency restriction? The only alternative open to them in these circumstances is to use smuggled currency and enrich national and international racketeers and crook who prey upon our financial and economic difficulties.

No independent African State today by itself has a chance to follow an independent course of economic development, and many of us who have tried to do this have been almost ruined or have had to return to the fold of the former colonial rulers. This position will not change unless we have a unified policy working at the continental level. The first step towards our cohesive economy would be a unified monetary zone, with, initially, an agreed common parity for our currencies. To facilitate this arrangement, Ghana would change to a decimal system. When we find that the arrangement of a fixed common parity is working successfully, there would seem to be no reason for not instituting one common currency and a single bank of issue. With a common currency from one common bank of issue we should be able to stand erect on our own feet because such an arrangement would be fully backed by the combined national products of the states composing the union. After all, the purchasing power of money depends on productivity and the productive exploitation of the natural, human and physical resources of the nation.

While we are assuring our stability by a common defence

system, and our economy is being orientated beyond foreign control by a Common Currency, Monetary Zone and Central Bank of Issue, we can investigate the resources of our continent. We can begin to ascertain whether in reality we are the richest, and not, as we have been taught to believe, the poorest among the continents. We can determine whether we possess the largest potential in hydroelectric power, and whether we can harness it and other sources of energy to our own industries. We can proceed to plan our industrialisation on a continental scale, and to build up a common market for nearly three hundred million people.

Common Continental Planning for the Industrial and Agricultural Development of Africa is a vital necessity.

So many blessings must flow from our unity; so many disasters must follow on our continued disunity, that our failure to unite today will not be attributed by posterity only to faulty reasoning and lack of courage, but to our capitulation before the forces of neo-colonialism and imperialism.

The hour of history which has brought us to this assembly is a revolutionary hour. It is the hour of decision. For the first time, the economic imperialism which menaces us is itself challenged by the irresistible will of our people.

The masses of the people of Africa are crying for unity. The people of Africa call for the breaking down of the boundaries that keep them apart. They demand an end to the border disputes between sister African states—disputes that arise out of the artificial barrier raised by colonialism. It was colonialism's purpose that divided us. It was colonialism's purpose that left us with our border irredentism, that rejected our ethnic and cultural fusion.

Our people call for unity so that they may not lose their patrimony in the perpetual service of neo-colonialism. In their fervent push for unity, they understand that only its realisation will give full meaning to their freedom and our African independence.

It is this popular determination that must move us on to a Union of Independent African States. In delay lies danger to our well-being, to our very existence as free states. It has been suggested that our approach to unity should be gradual, that it should be piece-meal. This point of view conceives of Africa as a static entity with "frozen" problems which can be eliminated one by one and when all have been cleared then we can come together and say: "Now all is well. Let us now unite." This view takes no account of the impact of external pressures. Nor does it take cognisance of the danger that delay can deepen our isolations and exclusiveness; that it can enlarge our differences and set us drifting further and further apart into the net of neo-colonialism, so that our union will become nothing but a fading hope, and the great design of Africa's full redemption will be lost, perhaps, forever.

The view is also expressed that our difficulties can be resolved simply by a greater collaboration through co-operative association in our inter-territorial relationships. This way of looking at our problems denies a proper conception of their inter-relationship and mutuality. It denies faith in a future for African advancement in African independence. It betrays a sense of solution only in continued reliance upon external sources through bilateral agreements for economic and other forms of aid.

The fact is that although we have been co-operating and associating with one another in various fields of common endeavour even before colonial times, this has not given us the continental identity and the political and economic force which would help us to deal effectively with the complicated problems confronting us in Africa today. As far as foreign aid is concerned, a United Africa would be in a more favourable position to attract assistance from foreign sources. There is the far more compelling advantage which this arrangement offers, in that aid will come from anywhere to a united Africa because our bargaining power would become infinitely greater. We shall no longer be dependent upon aid from restricted sources.

What are we looking for in Africa? Are we looking for Charters, conceived in the light of the United Nations example? A type of United Nations Organisation whose decisions are framed on the basis of resolutions that in our experience have sometimes been ignored by member States? Where groupings are formed and pressures develop in accordance with the interests of the groups concerned?

Or is it intended that Africa should be turned into a loose organisation of States on the model of the Organisation of American States, in which the weaker States within it can be at the mercy of the stronger or more powerful ones politically or economically and all at the mercy of some powerful outside nation or group of nations? Is this the kind of association we want for ourselves in th United Africa we all speak of with such feeling and emotion?

Your Excellencies, permit me to ask: Is this the kind of framework we desire for our United Africa? An arrangement which in future could permit Ghana or Nigeria or the Sudan, or Liberia, or Egypt or Ethiopia for example, to use pressure, which either superior economic or political influence gives, to dictate the flow and direction of trade from, say, Burundi or Togo or Nyasaland to Mozambique or Madagascar?

We all want a united Africa, united not only in our concept of what unity connotes, but united in our common desire to move forward together in dealing with all the problems that can best be solved only on a continental basis.

When the first Congress of the United States met many years ago in Philadelphia one of the delegates sounded the first chord of unity by declaring that they had met in "a state of nature." In other words, they were not in Philadelphia as Virginians, or Pensylvanians, but simply as Americans. This reference to themselves as Americans was in those days a new and strange experience. May I dare to assert equally on this occasion Your Excellencies, that we meet there today not as Ghanaians, Guineans, Egyptians, Algerians, Moroccans, Malians, Liberians, Congolese or Nigerians but as Africans. Africans united in our resolve to remain here until we have agreed on the basic principles of a new compact of unity among ourselves which guarantees for us and our future a new arrangement of continental government.

If we succeed in establishing a New Set of Principles as the basis of a New Charter or Statute for the establishment of a continental our people, then, in my view, this conference should mark the end of our various groupings and regional blocs. But if we fail and let this grand and historic opportunity slip by then we shall give way to greater dissension and vision among us for which the people of Africa will never forgive us. And the popular and progressive forces and movements within Africa will condemn us. I am sure therefore that we shall not fail them.

I have spoken at some length, Your Excellencies, because it is necessary for us all to explain not only to one another present here but also to our people who have entrusted to us the fate and destiny of Africa. We must therefore not leave this place until we have set up effective machinery for achieving African Unity. To this end, I now propose for your consideration the following:-

As a first step, Your Excellencies, a declaration of principle uniting and binding us together and to which we must all faithfully and loyally adhere, and laying the foundations of unity should be set down. And there should also be a formal declaration that all the Independent African States here and now agree to the establishment of a Union of African States.

As a second and urgent step for the realisation of the unification of Africa, an All-Africa Committee of Foreign Ministers be set up now, and that before we rise from this Conference a date should be fixed for them to meet.

This Committee should establish on behalf of the Heads of our governments a permanent body of officials and experts to work out a machinery for the Union Government of Africa. This body of officials and experts should be made up of two of the best brains from each independent African State. The various Charters of the existing groupings and other relevant documents could also be submitted to the officials and experts. A Presidium consisting of the heads of Governments of the Independent African States should be called upon to meet and adopt a Constitution and other recommendations which will launch the Union Government of Africa.

We must also decide on a location where this body of officials and experts will work as the new Headquarters or Capital of our Union Government. Some central place in Africa might be the fairest suggestion either at Bangui in the Central African Republic of Leopoldville in Congo. My Colleagues may have other proposals. The Committee of Foreign Ministers, officials and experts should be empowered to establish:

(1) a Commission to frame a constitution for a Union

Government of African States;

(2) a Commission to work out a continent-wide plan for a unified or common economic and industrial programme for Africa; this plan should include proposals for setting up:

(a) A Common Market for Africa;

(b) An African Currency;

(c) African Monetary Zone;

(d) An African Central Bank, and

(e) A continental Communication system.

(3) a Commission to draw up details for a Common Foreign Policy and Diplomacy.

(4) a Commission to produce plans for a Common System of Defence.

(5) a Commission to make proposals for a Common African Citizenship.

These Commissions will report to the Committee of Foreign Ministers who should in turn submit within six months of this Conference their recommendations to the Presidium. The Presidium meeting in Conference at the Union Headquarters will consider and approve the recommendations of the Committee of Foreign Ministers.

In order to provide funds immediately for the work of the permanent officials and experts of the Headquarters of the Union, I suggest that a special Committee be set up to work out a budget for this.

Your Excellencies, with these steps, I submit, we shall be irrevocably committed to the road which will bring us to a Union Government for Africa. Only a United Africa with central political direction can successfully give effective material and moral support to our freedom fighters, in Southern Rhodesia, Angola, Mozambique, Portuguese Guinea, etc., and of course South Africa. All Africa must be liberated now. It is therefore imperative for us here and now to establish a liberation bureau for African freedom fighters. The main object of this bureau, to which all governments should subscribe, should be to accelerate the emancipation of the rest of Africa still under colonial and racialist domination and oppression. It should be our joint responsibility to finance and support this bureau. On their successful attainment of Independence these territories will automatically join our Union of African States, and thus strengthen the fabric of Mother Africa. We shall leave here, having laid the foundation for our unity.

Your Excellencies, nothing could be more fitting than that the unification of Africa should be born on the soil of the State which stood for centuries as the symbol of African Independence.

Let us return to our people of Africa not with empty hands and with high-sounding resolutions, but with the firm hope and assurance that at long last African Unity has become a reality. We shall thus begin the triumphant march to the kingdom of the African Personality, and to a continent of prosperity, and progress, of equality and justice and of work and happiness. This shall be our victory—victory within a continental government of a Union of African States. This victory will give our voice greater force in world affairs and enable us to throw our weight more forcibly on the side of peace. The world needs peace in which the greatest advantage can be taken of the benefits of science and technology. Many of the world's present ills are to be found in the insecurity and fear engendered by the threat of nuclear war. Especially do the new nation need peace in order to make their way into a life of economic and social well-being amid an atmosphere of security and stability that will promote moral, cultural and spiritual fulfilment.

If we in Africa can achieve the example of a continent knit together in common policy and common purpose, we shall have made the f nest possible contribution to that peace for which all men and women thirst today, and which will lift once and forever the deepening shadow of global destruction from mankind. Ethiopia shall STRETCH forth her hands unto God.

AFRICA MUST UNITE

11

CLOSING REMARKS AFTER SIGNING OF O. A. U. CHARTER

Addis Ababa
May 25, 1963

YOUR IMPERIAL MAJESTY, MR. CHAIRMAN, YOUR EXCELLENCIES, BROTHERS AND FRIENDS,

We have come to the end of a historic and momentous Conference. The decisions we have taken here have made African Unity a reality and we can see clearly a Union Government of Africa in the horizon.

This is the goal which we set ourselves when we struggled in our separate States for Independence. It is also the compelling force which brought us together in Addis Ababa.

As I have said over and over again, the independence of our separate State is meaningless, unless the whole of Africa becomes free and united.

The resolutions we have made here are a symbol of our determination to become united and to remain united in an African Community with common aspirations and common objectives.

Freedom Fighters in all parts of our Continent can now be assured that they are not alone in their struggle. The whole weight and power of a united Africa is behind them.

After centuries of colonial exploitation and domination Africa has been re-born. We have discovered our common identity, a force with which we can re-assert our African personality.

We shall from now on think, plan and work together for the progress and development of our great Continent. In this way, we shall eliminate completely the handicaps, set-backs and humiliation we have suffered under colonialism and imperialism.

We should be happy that at long last by the adoption of this

Charter, we have seen the end of the various groupings and regional blocs.

It only remains for me, Your Majesty, on behalf of my colleagues and myself, to convey to the Government and people of Ethiopia especially to His Imperial Majesty, my sincere expression of gratitude for a happy and memorable stay in Addis Ababa.

The ancient Greeks identified Ethiopia with the Black Race. I would therefore like to leave with you a little poem on this:

Ethiopia Shall Rise

Ethiopia, Africa's bright gem,
Set high among the verdant hills
That gave birth to the unfailing
Waters of the Nile;
Ethiopia shall rise,
Ethiopia, bold craddle of Africa's ancient rule
And fertile School
of our African culture;
Ethiopia the wise
Shall rise
And remould with us the full figure
Of Africa's hopes
And destiny.

12

ON ARRIVAL
AT ACCRA AIRPORT

Accra
May 27, 1963

A week ago, I left Accra for Addis Ababa to attend the Conference of Heads of State and Government of the Independent African States. You will recall that in 1958, exactly five years ago, when the first Conference of Independent African States was held in Accra, there were only eight Independent States in Africa. At this Conference in Addis Ababa, there were representatives from thirty-one independent African States. All of us at this Conference were unanimous in our determination to lay concrete foundations for the freedom and unity of Africa.

I am happy to inform you that as a result of the work we did in Addis Ababa we have created a Continental Organisation of African Unity. This Charter for the Organisation of African Unity will soon be presented to Parliament for ratification. A major outcome of the Addis Ababa Conference is that the existing blocs and political groupings in Africa have come to an end. There is now only one Africa with a common aspiration and common objective.

Countrymen, in spite of the manoeuvres and intrigues of the colonialists and their agents, the unity of the African Continent has become a reality. After years of colonial exploitation and oppression, Africa has been re-born. From now on, we have a common identity and a common destiny.

I am sure that we in Ghana will support and sustain this Union of African States with the same zeal and determination with which we carried out the struggle for our independence.

On the eve of our independence, I stated that the independence of Ghana is meaningless unless it is linked up with the total liberation of the whole of the African Continent. With our united force in

Africa, we are now in a stronger position to assist our brothers who are still fighting for their freedom auld independence. Very soon they too will be free and unite with us. This imposes on all of us a greater obligation to work harder and more zealously not only for Ghana but for all Africa.

Friends and Countrymen, African Unity has become a reality. I can now see the Union Government of Africa already here.

The atmosphere at Addis Ababa Conference was most cordial and we all parted happy and determined. Personally, I have never felt happier. The political unification of Africa which has been my life-long dream is now almost here.

Friends and Countrymen, I thank you very much for the kind messages and good wishes which you sent to me at Addis Ababa. I thank you also for this very warm and cordial reception.

13

THIRD ANNIVERSARY OF GHANA YOUNG PIONEERS

Accra
June 14, 1963

On the occasion of the Third Anniversary of the Young Pioneer Movement, I am happy to send to all of you in the Movement my hearty congratulations.

I have followed with admiration the progress of the Young Pioneer Movement and its efforts to inculcate in the youth of Ghana the virtues of courage, humility and service to the community.

Today, only six years after the Independence of Ghana, a solid foundation has been laid for the political unification of Africa. A great responsibility therefore rests on the youth of Ghana and Africa. Indeed, they should feel proud to be alive today and to be playing a worthy part in the historical revolution of Africa.

The youth of Ghana should stand together in singleness of purpose in order to meet loyally and boldly this supreme challenge of our time. We can no longer afford to see the energies of our youth dissipated, and their loyalties confused, as a result of protracted membership of a variety of organisations, the aims and policies of which, however worthy they may be, are not always in our national or cultural interest.

For this reason, the programmes and training schemes of all such Youth Organisations established in Ghana should be harmonised so that our young men and women can keep faith with African nationalism and grow up in comradeship, honesty, integrity and devoted service in keeping with our African traditions. In this way, we can be sure that they will uphold the dignity of Africa and the African personality, cultivate a proper spirit of service, love for work and adventure, and aspire to the highest standards of responsibility and discipline.

I have directed accordingly that it be made compulsory for all

Youth Organisations throughout Ghana to participate fully in the Leadership Courses and other training schemes organised by the Young Pioneer Movement throughout the country. This, I am sure, will yield immense benefits to all concerned.

May the Young Pioneers and all the Youth Organisations in Ghana continue to prosper with each succeeding year.

14

FOURTEENTH ANNIVERSARY OF THE CONVENTION PEOPLE'S PARTY

Accra

MY DEAR PARTY COMRADES AND COUNTRYMEN,

Today marks the fourteenth year of the birth of our Party and I take this opportunity to salute all Party Comrades for their sustained effort and solidarity, their heroic struggle and vigilance throughout the years of our existence as a Party.

As we celebrate this Anniversary today, it is useful once again to re-examine our position and analyse the present stage of the struggle. Before we do so, however, let us, as usual bow our heads in a minute's silence and remember all those comrades of our dear Party who gave up their lives in the cause of our country's freedom.

On previous Anniversary occasions, we have recounted the glorious history of our Party, the strategy and tactics which it adopted to circumvent and rout Colonialism in Ghana. Although the struggle continues unabated, I must point out that the emphasis of the struggle has now shifted to the African scene and I crave your indulgence to turn to this sphere before coming home to our internal affairs, as this anniversary follows closely on the historic Addis Ababa Conference. You all remember what I said on the declaration of our Independence in 1957, namely: "That the independence of Ghana is meaningless unless it is linked up with the total liberation of the African Continent."

These words form the cornerstone of our Foreign Policy.

In April, 1958, a Conference of Independent African States was held here at which date there were only 8 Independent African State.

Today as I have said, following subsequent Conferences organised on our initiative in pursuance of our policy there are 3 Independent African States. This phenomenal rise in the number of Independent States of Africa is a vindication of the correctness of our African

Policy. It also shows the soundness of our philosophy on the African liberation Movement and African Unity.

A new period has opened in contemporary African history with the convening of the Addis Ababa Conference, a period in which the peoples of Africa have demonstrated their revolutionary determination to forge a common indissoluble link in shaping their collective effort to the collective advantage of their own peoples. The realisation of this noble aim is a hopeful step in the consolidation of world peace, because the existence of colonialism in all its forms in Africa and for that matter anywhere in the world constitutes a threat to world peace.

We live in an age when the peoples of Africa are resolutely throwing off the abominable yoke of colonialism, in order to organise their national economies in the paramount interest of their peoples after centuries of foreign unjust domination.

The theme of Addis Ababa was the unity of the African Peoples in order to attain the overwhelming economic, financial and cultural advantage which lie readily available to all of us upon our unity. What I have striven to emphasise is that although political independence has been proclaimed, the struggle for independence still continues because political independence is not the end; it is a means to an end.

Our political independence must be used to raise the standard of living of our peoples. But our concrete African conditions demand that all African states should work together for the consolidation of their gains in the liberation of our people. We can survive only within the context of African Unity and independence.

Now I turn to Party Organisation. The new tasks of the Party at the present stage of the struggle coupled with the role which our country plays in international affairs make it necessary for the organisation of our Party to be streamlined and strengthened to enable it to cope with the new responsibilities Ghana is committed to discharge. Accordingly, our Party must ever be concerned with multiplying and strengthening its contacts with the masses of the people and winning their confidence as their defenders against the evils of poverty, disease, hunger, ignorance and squalor to whose elimination we are dedicated.

The Party gains strength with the masses if it practises inner Party democracy and self-criticism. All members of our Party should be encouraged in every possible way to take active part in discussing all major questions of Party life. If this is done, it will follow conclusively that all decisions of the Party are decisions of the entire membership who will correctly understand and appreciate them. Democracy will then be at its plenitude throughout all the levels of our Party. I must once again emphasise that the masses of the people form the backbone of our Party and their living conditions and their welfare must be paramount in everything we do. It is for them in particular and Africa in general that our Party exists. So much for our tact with the masses of the people.

To achieve the foregoing objectives, there is a clear need to so reorganise the Party that it touches every single individual wherever he or she may live in order not only to bring the entire people into participation in the administration of the country but also to make it impossible to external and internal reactionaries and their agents to interfere with the security of our State and the progress being made in all sphere of our national life. Our Party has shown by its victory over Colonialism and all its new forms in our dear land that it can cope with any situation for which it prepares itself and we must fortify our ranks with mass vigilance to deal a death-blow at subversion and other un-Ghanaian activities wherever they may rear their ugly head. For this reason, the Party must now base its organisation on reaching the people directly by house to-house and street by street method all over the country, so that we may chase out the enemy, routing him without giving him a moment's rest to re-group his forces.

Our Party's new down-to-earth organisation will also enable our development work to be tackled more forcefully and on mass basis, as we shall be able to bring everyone into useful local activity.

As I have written elsewhere, I will not hide the fact that I am impatient when it comes to building Ghana, and this task rests on the shoulders of my colleagues in Government. We have to get on with the job resolutely in order to fulfil our promises to the people. Each Minister must regard himself as a managing director and get his particular job done in the allotted time, and properly done. Success follows organisation and inauguration. Real difficulties leading to legitimate delay always receive understanding consideration. But the driving urge to succeed must permeate every branch of government, steaming from the ministerial fountain-head, who must combine a high sense of responsibility with a high sense of urgency. Ministers and Party officials must show themselves as examples to the people by their devotion to their work, by simple living, by leading in service.

Ghana faces immense difficulties in her task of reconstruction. It is by no means a simple business to raise educational levels, to train skilled workers and to impart a sense of responsibility speedily especially in circumstances of restricted availability of local qualified personnel and material resources. Nevertheless, there is much that can be done quickly if everyone puts every ounce of ability and strength into the building of the nation. It is a prime task of leadership in Ghana to make the people aware of the compelling need to put forth their most intense effort on behalf of the progress of the country and of themselves.

A new stage is set for Party ideological education. Every Party member must now be educated to understand precisely what the Party stands for. The philosophy of our Party, which had led to victory over Colonialism in our country and which governs our international relations or more particularly our relations with other African countries, has been proved sound and correct through its application in practice the concrete situation in Africa. This philosophy has been profusely propounded in various forms and underlines our Party Programme for Work and Happiness, the systematic study of which is a full realisation of Party education. In our Programme for Work and Happiness is embodied the concrete results of our political awakening and ideological understanding. To understand the ideology of our Party is to appreciate the need to improve the well-being of the greatest number of the people.

May God give us peace in our time to work for the welfare of the people of Ghana, Africa and the world.

15

RATIFICATION OF THE O. A. U. CHARTER

The National Assembly
June 21, 1963

I am here to invite you to ratify the Charter of African Unity adopted by the Addis Ababa Conference. This meeting of the Heads of State and Government of the existing Independent African States has rightly been acclaimed as the most momentous event in Africa's modern history. Addis Ababa will certainly be recorded as a crucial turning point in our struggle against the final bastions of colonialism in Africa and as the founding place of Continental African Union.

The Charter adopted at Addis Ababa enjoins us all to go forward in unity. This Charter, the Charter of the Organization of African Unity, which I signed along with all the other Heads Of State and Government of the Independent African States, and which has been placed before the House for ratification, contains the will and determination of our countries to achieve the unity of our Continent.

The coming together on a basis of unity of all the Independent African States has created a new factor in the fight against imperialism and its twin instruments of colonialism and neo-colonialism. Our combined strength are to be placed at the service of our brothers waging an all-out struggle against oppressive colonialism in all those parts of our continent still under alien domination. We have covenanted together to co-ordinate and harmonise our general policies in the sphere of our political, diplomatic, economic, educational, cultural, health, scientific and technical activities, as well as in the sphere of defence and security.

There are wide enough areas of mutual co-operation that should lead us to a Centralised Continental Union and give effective protection to our sovereign Independence.

The Charter of African Unity must be regarded as the last but one step on the road to a Continental Union. Its provisions certainly challenge foreign political and economic domination of our Continent. The exploiters of Africa have grasped its implications. They realise that we are out to make ourselves masters in our own house and to drive out relentlessly from the length and breadth of our Continent those forces which batten upon us and keep us in political and economic subjection.

A Provisional Secretariat has been set up with a Provisional Headquarters at Addis Ababa. The Secretariat is composed of the representatives of Ghana, Nigeria, Egypt, Ethiopia, Niger and Uganda.

One of the major decisions of the Addis Ababa Conference is the setting up of a Co-ordinating Committee with Headquarters at Dar-es-Salaam in Tanganyika. This Committee will be responsible for regulating the assistance from African States and for managing the special fund which is being created by contributions from all the Independent African Governments.

This means that we must accept as our primary task the extension of independence to all territories of Africa. Apart from the sense of oneness and unity which impels us to go to the aid of our suffering compatriots in Angola, Mozambique, Southern Rhodesia, South Africa, and other parts of Africa still under colonial rule, we know that none of the Independent African States is safe so long as a single colonial ruler remains on African soil.

Freedom Fighters will take renewed hope and determination from the knowledge that their struggle is identified with the continued independence of the existing African States and is to be directed within a total strategy. No longer will these Freedom Fighters who have been on the vanguard of the African revolution and the colonial liberation movement feel isolated from the mainstream of African independence and unity. I am indeed happy that the goal which we set ourselves at our independence has been brought nearer. We shall strive for it now, not alone, but with our brothers from all the Independent African States.

Speaking of the liberation and unity of our Continent, I may mention that there are two main categories of Freedom Fighters:

(a) those fighting in colonial territories for the overthrow of exploitation and oppression by foreign governments: and

(b) those who consider that they have a duty to fight in order to strengthen the independence of their countries where colonial rule has been overthrown, but where it is still necessary to create conditions for the welfare of the people and for the elimination of neo-colonialist interference and influence.

As long as conditions in these countries are such as to assist the maintenance of neo-colonialism, discontent cannot be stifled or suppressed. The governments of such countries are a menace, no only to their own states but also to the safety and security of our entire continent.

The Government of Ghana fully appreciates the right of any State to grant political asylum to such Fighters under the accepted conventions of international law, it also appreciates that, unless conditions in their states change radically in the interest and welfare of the masses of the people, such Freedom Fighters cannot but resort to the use of constitutional, or even revolutionary, methods and activities aimed at securing a change of regime in their countries.

Most of these nationalists have sought refuge in African countries, other than their own, as a result of their struggle against neo-colonialism. We have quite a few of them in Ghana. There are others in other parts of Africa. We did not invite them here, but they naturally felt that they could enjoy sanctuary and be given the necessary protection in Ghana which has for the past six years since her attainment of independence and sovereignty played host to Freedom Fighters from all over the continent. The African Affairs Centre in Accra is a symbol of this determination.

These nationalists, some of whom were stalwart warriors in the struggle against colonialism, were received and accorded the traditional African and Ghanaian hospitality not as criminals fleeing from justice, but as victims of persecution by the neo-colonialists and their agents. But, Mr. Speaker, at the Addis Ababa Conference, all the signatories to the Charter of African Unity solemnly pledged themselves to fight colonialism, neo-colonialism and imperialism in all its forms.

In order, therefore, to preserve the spirit of unity so happily engendered at Addis Ababa, I consider it essential that we should declare publicly the principles that must henceforth govern our granting of political asylum in Ghana to such refugees. These I set forth as follows:-

(a) Ghanaians and the nationals of the Independent African States are kinsmen and brothers and must be hospitable to one another. If, for any reason, such compatriots leave their territories the bond of fraternity that exists between us and their people makes it incumbent on Ghana to grant them hospitality.

(b) However, such hospitality cannot continue unless they observe the following conditions:

(i) the Government and the institutions which have been established by the will of the people in their respective territories, in accordance with the constitution freely chosen by them, must be respected;

(ii) they will be free to work in Ghana and earn their living here, but in no case can the Government of Ghana give them any material assistance, inasmuch as the Independent African States now maintain a central fund for the granting of such assistance to Freedom Fighters;

(iii) as long as the refugees remain in Ghana, they are forbidden to do anything whatsoever against the Government and the institutions of their country.

It is our earnest hope and belief that our own example in the creation of a Socialist pattern of Society, in which the free development of each is a condition for the free development of all is bound to have a striking impact on regimes in Africa in which the wealth and resources of the people are concentrated in the hands of neo-colonialists and their agents.

Now, Mr. Speaker, Members of the National Assembly, in order to complete the liberation of our Continent, we must face the problem of South Africa and of Portuguese colonies on the Continent.

The arms which the Portuguese colonialists use in Angola and Mozambique, the bombs which they dropped in Senegal, were not manufactured in Portugal, nor were they paid for by Portugal. Portugal is the poorest State in Europe and the average Ghanaian, as our statistics show, is now wealthier than the average citizen of Portugal. Portugal by herself could not for a year continue to maintain the vast military apparatus which she employs for the suppression of the people and the exploitation of the resources of large areas of the African Continent.

Ghana has no quarrel in principle with the various treaty arrangements which States outside Africa make to secure their own defence, except where they impinge upon the sovereignty of Independent African States and the desire of the colonial territories in Africa to accede to independence. No one in Ghana could justifiably question, for instance, the avowed purpose of the North Atlantic Treaty Organization as set out in the words of its preamble, which I quote to you:

> "The parties to this treaty reaffirm their faith in the purposes and principles of the United Nations and their desire to live in peace with all peoples and all governments. They are determined to safeguard the freedom, common heritage, and civilisation of their peoples, founded on the principles of democracy, individual liberty, and the rule of law. They seek to promote stability and well-being in the North Atlantic area. They are resolved to unite their efforts for collective defence for the preservation of peace and security. They therefore agree to this North Atlantic Treaty."

But Angola and Mozambique are no part of North Atlantic defence. The Portuguese in Africa are not defending the freedom, common heritage, or civilisation of the African people. They observe no principle of democracy, no individual liberty, nor the rule of law. In its conduct in Africa, Portugal acts continuously in defiance of the purposes and principles of the United Nations. Yet the truth is that NATO weapons and NATO support alone enable Portugal to survive as a colonial power in African even today.

I am certain that the moral case against NATO support for Portugal while she remains an oppressor of the African people, is so strong and overwhelming that the NATO powers must have no alternative but to withdraw their support. Appeals from individual African States may be passed over, unheeded. But the voice of a united Africa cannot go unheeded.

Portugal, unfortunately, is not the only colonial power which still retains control of African territory. With the exception of Madagascar and two small islands—one off the coast of Guinea and the other off the coast of Ethiopia—every single island belonging to the African continent is still a colonial possession. On the African Continent itself, in addition to Portugal, Spain and France still maintain colonial possession, and a large area of African territory is still under British colonial rule.

As I have said time and again, colonialism is an anachronism today and these various powers must give up their colonial possessions with grace and retire honourably. It is therefore with joy that we hail the beginning of the ending of the long struggle against colonialism in Kenya and applaud the successful conclusion of the recent; elections there in favour of KANU. We equally rejoice at the clear; prospect of independence for Nyasaland and Northern Rhodesia.

But Mr. Speaker, it is the future of Southern Rhodesia which casts such a dark cloud on the horizon of Africa's freedom and independence.

Let us make our position perfectly clear on this vital issue. In the past, Britain, by force of arms, imposed upon the people of Southern Rhodesia or, to give it its natural, indigenous name, Zambia, an alien government designed to deprive the people of Zambia of their lands and their mineral wealth. Britain was a party to the establishment of a government composed exclusively of minority settlers who had, contrary to all conceptions of justice, possessed themselves of the lands and resources of the inhabitants. This settler government of Southern Rhodesia is now demanding that it should be granted independence. In other words, it is inviting the British Government to set up a second South Africa in the heart of our Continent without taking into account the wishes of the majority of the people in that territory.

No African States could in any way accept such a travesty of morality, justice and international law. Nor would we accept the undemocratic, racialist counter-proposals which the British Government is reported to have made to the settler Southern Rhodesian Government. Any Government that is formed in Southern Rhodesia without the consent of the majority of its people will be unacceptable. Not only would we refuse to acknowledge any such government; we shall oppose its entry into the Commonwealth and into the United Nations. Our recognition will only go to a Government which in our view is fully representative of the people of Zambia. That is, a Government based upon universal adult suffrage, employing the principle of one man one vote.

You will recall, Mr. Speaker, Members of the National Assembly, that on the very threshold of our independence, the British Government compelled us to go to the polls more than once to prove to the world that the Convention People's Party enjoyed the fullest support of the majority of our people. The independence of Nigeria was similarly delayed in order that the British Government might satisfy itself that all sections of the population were properly represented in Parliament. Kenya had to endure a similar election for the same reason.

In all these cases, the United Kingdom Government sought to justify its position by maintaining that its actions were based on its avowed dedication to the principles of democracy and representative government. Let me ask now, Mr. Speaker, what makes the case of Southern Rhodesia different from the pre-independence situation in Ghana, Nigeria and Kenya? There is no need to pause for a reply.

I cannot believe that any British Government could commit the supreme folly and blunder of setting up at this stage of our African struggle for independence and unity a second South Africa, whose examples of the appalling evils of apartheid and minority rule are so glaringly manifested against the African population every single day. I have left the British Government in no doubt about the stand we are prepared to take against the setting up of an unpopular minority independent Government of Southern Rhodesia.

This is a crucial and decisive moment in the history of Southern Africa. The attainment of political freedom by the people of

Southern Rhodesia would not only mean the setting up of a free and indigenous Zambian state. It would bring a message of hope and encouragement to African people elsewhere in Southern Africa who are denied any right to control their own affairs. But Zambia will, in any event, become free.

In truth, of course, the situation in Southern Rhodesia could have been solved as has been the Kenya situation, but for one factor—the proximity of Southern Rhodesia to South Africa. Indeed, the Southern Rhodesian settlers are nothing more than pawns in the game of chess now being played by the Foreign powers over South Africa. The independence of the people of Southern Rhodesia is not in reality being considered on its merits. It is considered only in relation to the South African situation.

South Africa is the biggest impediment to the liberation and unity of the African Continent, and it is a question which we must face squarely and realistically.

For sometime now we have tried a line of policy, namely, that if only one was patient and negotiated and tried to understand the problems of South Africa, then the situation would gradually begin to improve, and little by little racial oppression would disappear.

However, Mr. Speaker, our experience has proved this policy to be false. The sincerity of our approach can be judged from the fact that South Africa was invited to the first Conference of Independent African States here in Accra. It is of some significance that she, refused to attend unless the other colonial powers were invited as well. We attempted to exchange High Commissioners; we met with South African whites at various African and international Conferences, and we tried in every way to follow a path of persuasion and conciliation. Our efforts were entirely without results, and I think it is now clear to everyone that the South African situation cannot be dealt with by attempts to maintain the normal channels of diplomatic and commercial association, or by appeals to morality and religion, justice and codes of ethics.

Unfortunately, the great powers, and some of the smaller ones, still continue to export arms to South Africa. Have those who have authorised the export of such arms made any enquiry as to the real purpose for which they are required by South Africa? Have they asked why so many small arms should be needed for the protection of South African whites? For what purpose do these States consider that Apartheid South Africa requires aircraft capable of and designed for carrying nuclear rockets and weapons? The Buccaneer aircraft with its limited range and about which there has recently been controversy in Britain is not such as could be employed against, say, the Soviet Union, or the United States of America or indeed against any State outside the African Continent. Against whom on the African Continent, then, are they intended to be employed?

These are questions all the Independent African States are asking and would like to have answered. But we would be helping the cause of the world peace if the traffic in arms to South Africa were stopped. In the spirit and context of the Addis Ababa resolutions, I have instructed the Ghanaian representative on the Security Council to raise immediately as a matter of urgency with his African colleagues the question as to whether the United Nations should not call upon all nations to cease forthwith to supply arms to South Africa.

The decisions taken at Addis Ababa demand the breaking off of diplomatic and consular relations between all the African States and the Governments of Portugal and South Africa. They call for an effective boycott of foreign trade with the two countries. It is for all the Independent African States to see that their total economic and political boycott is made complete without delay. The allies of the colonial powers have also been given notice that they must choose between their friendship for the African peoples and their support of the powers that oppress African peoples. This reflects as well upon those countries which have accepted as a political principle the independence of colonial peoples, but which at times betray this principle out of expediency.

If the great powers, or even a large enough body of the smaller ones, were to support us by joining the boycott, the moral effect would have tremendous repercussions throughout the African Continent, besides serving notice on the Verwoerd and Salazar regimes that they can no longer continue a policy of racial segregation, oppression and genocide. Surely, it must be obvious to every reasonable person that no minority settlers of European origin, can keep us indefinitely in subjection in our own continent. Is it not a staggering thought to think that in South Africa the law as established by a sheer minority of 3 million white settlers enables and permits them to control the destiny of 12 million of our people? Where is justice? Where is morality? Where is democracy? Let us not forget that, like the rest of the world the African Continent cannot exist, and refuses to exist, half free and half colonised.

Mr. Speaker and Members of the National Assembly, it is of great consequence that the States of the Organization of African Unity have, in Article Three of the Charter, solemnly affirmed and declared their adherence to the principle of a non-aligned policy.

Non-alignment is now a world factor and moral force in international relations. The contribution of Africa as a continent united in its observance of a truly non-aligned policy will give tremendous weight to that force. It will also give a great fillip to the search for permanent world peace.

Mr. Speaker, nothing has stood so firmly in the way of African freedom or hindered African unity as the existence of foreign bases on African soil and African involvement through military alliances and pacts with powers outside the African Continent. If we are to combine our forces and create a common strategy both in support of Africa's Freedom Fighters and in the defence and protection of our established independence, then it goes without saying that all such bases and all such pacts need to be annulled. Unless this is done, we stand exposed and our charter will remain nothing but a mere scrap of paper.

In saying this, I am not unmindful of the grave difficulties which face some of us. Lack of capital, economic weakness and political instability are conditions that have been responsible for the acceptance of economic and military dependence upon former colonial powers. In some instances such assistance is obtained not only for development, but even for meeting normal recurrent budgetary expenses. It is an act of high courage on the part of sister States thus boldly to have set their hand to a policy of non-alignment which can hardly be in keeping with the policy of those on whom, unhappily, they find themselves dependent.

Yet it is these States particularly that should find the greatest advantage in developing African Unity into a firmly welded concert of nations as a real political force with political direction under a central authority within which they can shed their economic and military dependence and retain their dignity. Proposals of aid need to be examined with care. Most of all we must beware of any kind of military help, for it can so easily place us in the hands of foreign powers and make them, in effect, the arbiters of our fate. Apart from drawing us into their orbit, they become intimately familiar with details of our defence structure and its strength. They can even become the designers of our defence structure and place us completely at their mercy. Aid of this kind, even where ostensibly free, can be most dangerous and costly in its consequences. For it creates pockets of cold-war presence on the African Continent and lets in the neo-colonialists with danger not only to the harbouring country but to its neighbours, to whom it poses an open threat. Above all, it creates frictions and disputes that disturb the unity upon which we have embarked and to which, I am convinced, all of us are sincerely dedicated. That is why it is so urgent for us to get together within a centralised framework that will give shape and purpose to the agreements which we made at Addis Ababa.

Co-ordination of our political and diplomatic policies, harmonisation of our economic, educational and cultural activities, collaboration in health, sanitation and nutritional matter, co-ordination in scientific and technical fields, co-operation for defence and security will go their dilatory pace unless the Organisation of African Unity is pivoted upon a centralised authority capable of giving effective political direction to these aims.

Political and diplomatic co-operation cannot function in a void. It needs some sort of a political constitution to direct it. Economic development in separate State is ineffective, but with our combined resources, governed by an overall plan, we can make Africa great, prosperous and progressive.

Above all, the full development of all our countries needs the most economic exploitation and husbanding of our natural and human resource. This is possible only on a continental scale, if we are to extract the greatest advantage from the latest industrial and administrative techniques as applied to our extensive land mass and population.

As a token of Ghana's dedication to the Charter of African Unity, I am setting on foot immediately plans for the exchange of students and for the provision at the University of Ghana of a course of studies in African Affairs and in History, Economics and Politics generally, which may be of value to other States who do not as yet possess universities in the training of their administrators. Educational and cultural co-operation in general demands effective co-ordination at inter-State level. A guide to the history of Africa should be produced to destroy once and for all the colonial myth that Africa has no past.

Mr. Speaker, the structure of the social organizations in our New Africa must embrace all sections of our people. The goals of our endeavours have always been to secure the material basis for increasing the economic and social wealth of our farmers, peasants and workers. Our revolution, therefore, must be identified with the organisations of the workers and our peasant population. We cannot succeed very much in our aims if there should be conflict between the trade unions as the organisation of the workers and our national Governments which are also serving the same interests. Our identical aims must make it possible for us to harmonise relations and work within a co-ordinated programme for solving the problems that face Africa.

The All-African Trade Union Federation must therefore be in a position to mobilise the exploited masses of Africa for the final onslaught in the battle against imperialism and neo-colonialism. In the Independent States of Africa, AATUF has a vital role to play in evolving a trade Union orientation which will enable the workers to play their full part in socialist construction.

An All-African Trade Union grouping independent of external conflicts can play a most useful part in fostering understanding within the International Labour Movement. International Labour Unity is essential for the preservation of peace and the security of mankind.

These, Mr. Speaker, are some of the implications of the Charter which I and the other Heads of State and Government signed at Addis Ababa. With goodwill and honest striving on the part of us all the Charter can become a reality within a workable Centralised African Union. In the march forward to our continental growth and prosperity, it is our earnest hope that the principle of the free development of each as a condition for the free development of all will find general acceptance in Africa. For it is within the functioning of this principle that it will be possible to smooth out those inequalities in our societies that engender social function and discontent imposed upon us by imperialism. We have arrived at national statehood in an epoch when the ordinary people will no longer tolerate the concentration of the national wealth and resources in the hands of a privileged few while the many go ragged, destitute and hungry. This is a factor of which we have to take full cognisance in designing our political, economic and social future, both at the national and continental levels. Otherwise we shall find ourselves in the sad position of stifling the hopes and aspirations of the vast masses of our people and being forced, in the face of their resentment and possible uprising, to resort to draconian measures which will sunder our societies and plunge us into civil strife, confusion and anarchy. Where such conditions arise, the neo-colonialists can enter unchecked to profit from them and menace the safety and security of our Continent.

This, then, is another most cogent argument for fashioning our African unity in a way that will bind us all closely in every field of endeavour and make the well-being and happiness of all our people its keynote. Only thus shall we achieve a calm and stable progress to that complete independence and unity which we desire to achieve in Africa.

With our continental liberation and unity, Africa will become a powerful force that will carry its total impact in the councils of the world. For that reason, no country in the world can afford to be indifferent to what we have set on foot at Addis Ababa.

Equally, in striving for African freedom and unity, we cannot be indifferent to events in other parts of the globe, which can vitally affect the progress which we make towards our goal. It is in this spirit that we have concerned ourselves about such grave international issues as the Sine-Indian border dispute and the Cuban situation. In doing so, we were not only serving the cause of world peace which is of vital importance to us. We were serving the cause of African liberation and unity as well.

I believe that the forces now pressing for freedom and unity in Africa will be strong enough to overcome any external obstacle. Yet we must not blind ourselves to the fact that one of the great causes of African disunity and of the maintenance of racialist and colonialist regimes on African soil is the disagreement and hostility which at present exists between the great powers.

Imperialism and the so-called white supremacy are the basic factors of instability in Africa and one of the contributory causes of world tension. Secondly, unless the situation in South Africa improves radically so to afford opportunities of the majority of the citizens of that State to express their will in a Government of their own, this could be a theatre for a world conflict. Racial oppression and injustice in any form cannot be condoned or ignored. Racialism is a blot on the conscience of mankind, and the sooner it is removed the greater the prospects of world peace will be. It is in the same context that one has to consider the problem of racial discrimination in the United States. Although the efforts now being made by the Government of the United States to bring about a solution to this long-standing problem in America are appreciated, it must be stated that nothing except a bold and revolutionary assault on this moral obloquy and this grave crisis of racial confidence in the United States, can bring about a speedy solution.

The Afro-American has been taught to appreciate the dignity of the individual, living as he does in one of the most technically advanced countries of our time; and yet at the same time he is being denied what is his essential and inalienable right. The Afro-American did not choose to go to the New World. He was dragged into America to help establish the economy of that country. This he has done with great credit, distinguishing himself in all fields of human endeavour. In Music, Law, Diplomacy, Art, Science, Education, he has achieved great distinction for America. The United States has therefore a moral duty to accept the essential humanity of the Afro-American.

Now, Mr. Speaker, let me turn to other problems that affect the position of the African and endanger world peace. The nuclear arms race in the Middle East is now an open secret. Instability in this area not only heightens world tension but jeopardises the security of the

African Continent. In the interests of world peace a way must therefore be found quickly to end the dangerous arms race between Israel and Egypt which could easily lead to disaster for Africa, the Middle East and the world. This arms race has already involved some of the major world powers who are aiding and abetting both sides in the struggle.

The world leaders must hasten to insulate the Middle East not only from the intensification of the Cold War crisis in that area but also from the threat of a nuclear arms clash between the Arabs and Israel. To this end, I have repeatedly called for a nuclear moratorium in the Middle East, for the creation of an Arab State for the refugees and for the permanent delimitation of the State of Israel. Time is running out, and I call again upon the United Nations to move as quickly as they can to save a very grave situation.

In the same way as the dispute between India and China over frontier delimitation heightens world tension and thus makes more difficult the tasks which we have set ourselves in Africa, so do the unhappy differences that have arisen between the United States and Cuba, which nearly sparked off a nuclear conflagration a few months ago. Whatever the causes of disagreement may be, the United States and Cuba must find a way to co-exist. Cuba has indicated her willingness of come to a settlement with the United States and to make appropriate restitution for United States assets nationalised by the Cuban Government. It would seem reasonable, therefore, for the United States which, in size, economic and military power, is far greater than Cuba, to express her greatness in an equal—if not greater—gesture of good will, magnanimity and statesmanship. Peaceful co-existence is essential and indispensable for the establishment of understanding between the nations at a time when nuclear weapons hang like the Sword of Damocles over the head of mankind.

Mr. Speaker, Members of the National Assembly, we can safeguard our independence and economic interests in Africa only if we speak with one voice. Only a united Africa can obtain capital on a large scale and technical aid from the industrially advanced countries without undue pressures and restrictive conditions. The only alternative I can see to this is confusion in our ranks, economic retrogression and a pitiful sell-out of our patrimony to the colonialists and imperialists.

Did we fight to secure sovereignty and independence only to exchange these precious attributes for a state of despair and despondency? We have proved at Addis Ababa that we are ready to build a united Africa, united in our conception of its importance and our common desire to move forward together in a triumphant march to the great kingdom of the African Personality, where although we may be Ghanaians, or Nigerians or Ethiopians, Algerians, Egyptians or Sierra Leonians, we shall have a common purpose and a common objective in working for the destiny of our Continent as Africans. Until Africa achieves total independence and national unification the African revolution will not have completed its destined task. When we talk of African Unity, we are thinking of a political arrangement which will enable us collectively to provide solutions for our problems in Africa.

Mr. Speaker, General de Gaulle is reported to have commented on the results achieved at the Addis Ababa Conference that the organisation of Africa which the Independent African States envisage is "a Federation of the various African regional grouping." What made him arrive at that conclusion, I cannot tell.

It is, however, a matter of great interest to us to observe that this Great European, now engrossed with his grand design for Europe, should feel such unsolicited concern for Africa. It should be quite clear to General de Gaulle that not only can he not be a greater African than the Africans themselves, but he cannot be both a Great European and a Great African.

Regional Grouping of any kind are a serious threat to the unity of Africa. Such groupings have decisive influences which can break the forces of cohesion and unity among us. General de Gaulle knows quite well that if regional federalism, this political commodity of dubious value, can be sold to Africa, the economic future of his Europe will be assured. Only by fomenting and nursing regional and sectional political groupings in Africa can the imperialists and ex-colonial powers be sure of retaining their rapidly waning influence in Africa. That is why, even after Addis Ababa, they wish to secure the political dismemberment of Africa. It is for the same reason that the British Government also is reported to have fervently supported the idea of a political federation in East Africa. This is surely timed to defeat the objectives of the Addis Ababa Conference. But all these manoeuvres will fail. Out of African Unity a new Africa will arise, life will be full and abundant; our culture and the arts, so long suppressed under colonial domination, will blossom again and flourish.

There can, therefore, be no co-existence between freedom and slavery on the African Continent, between African independence and colonial and neo-colonial domination, between Independent Africa and colonial imperialism. Such co-existence would mean denial of our African right to be free, a right as inalienable for us as for any other people of the world. It would be to condone the crime of apartheid, to accept the cruelties of Portuguese rule, to leave Africa at the mercy of even more ruthless suppression and exploitation. It would lay the independence of the sovereign African States wide open to the predatory attacks of the colonialists who still hold power in parts of our Continent. Africa would become a dark battleground of Western competitiveness that could only result in the miseries and horrors of open conflicts and civil wars.

Mr. Speaker, one of our great hopes in pursuing the goal of total African liberation and unity is the vista of world peace that it opens up. For the culmination of that goal we envisage the end of colonialism and neo-colonialism, the twin offspring of imperialism, the cause of much of the world's rivalry and divisions. Imperialism, which reached its zenith in the Western World in the period of capitalist democracy is finance capital and capitalist democracy run wild in other people's countries. Its first stage was during the period of direct political governance, known as colonialism. As colonialism is being forced to retreat under pressure of nationalist awakening the imperialists are making an all-out effort to consolidate and extend their domination by different means. These means are various and take on many forms; they can be direct or subtle. Mostly they are devious, often insinuating, frequently disguised. They may promise friendship or use political and economic blackmail. They add up to neo-colonialism, which is the last stage of imperialism in the epoch of rising independence among colonial peoples. With the widening of freedom's boundaries and the unification that now portends in Africa, the root of imperialism will undoubtedly weaken and it is difficult to forecast another stage to which it can go except to decline. But imperialism, colonialism and neo-colonialism will end only when conditions are such as to make their existence impossible. That is, when there are no nations and peoples exploiting others; when there are no vested interests exploiting the earth, it's fruits and resources for the benefit of a few against the well-being of the many. And I am convinced that our march in Africa towards total independence and unity must hasten this end and thereby add to The peace of the world.

This at once raises the matter of speed and urgency. Time is everything in our march. We must in Africa crowd into a generation the experience and achievements attained through centuries of trial and error by the older nations of the world. We do not wish to see Africa set on a course in which her nations grow in difficult, separate and competing directions until they develop into a confused and disorderly economic tangle of "Sixes and Sevens." Because Europe has become the victim of such economic circumstances that is surely no reason why Africa should follow a similar course. Those who set the example of Europe as an illustration for the need to develop step by step in Africa do not seem to appreciate that Africa need not begin by imitating the mistakes of Europe. After all, what use is the experience of human progress if we who study its course fail to learn from its errors and muddles. As I said at Addis Ababa, this world is no longer moving on camels and donkeys. Speed has become a new potent factor in the progress of the world. The progress of the modern man, like the agile Kangaroo, leaps and jumps.

More that that, we have to remove the gap between those nations and ourselves if we are to emerge from the grip of the economic imperialism that will retard us the longer it remains master, or even a part, of our economy. We have to keep in mind, however, that the gap is not a static one, but that it grows as modern technology improves and its productive capacities and output potentials increase. Thus the gap can widen seriously and new dangers threaten us, unless we hasten forward at a much accelerated speed. Consciousness of the time element among the leaders of Independent Africa was clearly revealed in the course of our deliberations at Addis Ababa. This awareness enabled us to examine our problems with a striking sense of urgency. It was responsible for the speed with which we were able to adopt a Charter of Unity for Africa.

Why, then, cannot we observe the same consciousness of time and the same sense of urgency, in pushing forward our unity into a form that will give it direction and authority, so that we can speed up our common development and advancement? In the horizon of Africa's future I see clearly the bright dawn of a Union Government, the birth of a great Nation which is no longer the dream of a new Utopia. Africa, the sleeping giant, is now awake and is coming into her very own.

Mr. Speaker, Members of the National Assembly, may Providence guide you and give you wise counsel in your deliberations.

16

OPENING OF
GOVERNMENT HOUSE

Osu, Accra
July 1, 1963

We have met here this afternoon for the formal opening of these beautiful extensions to the Castle which have recently been completed, and also to re-establish the Castle as the Permanent seat of administration of the Republic of Ghana. It is fitting that this ceremony should take place as part of the celebrations for the Third Anniversary of our Republic.

For many years before Ghana's independence, Christianborg Castle, as these buildings used to be called, was the home of the European Governors, and the seat of the colonial power. It was used before then, as a warehouse for the unfortunate men and women, who formed the merchandise in the abominable slave trade. It is recalled that in the year 1657, the Swedes built a Fortress at Osu on the site of an earlier Fort built by the Portuguese in 1578. In 1659, the Fort was captured by the Danes and named Christianborg Castle after King Christian the Fifth, the then King of Denmark.

We are told that in 1693, the Castle was captured by a brave Ghanaian by name Asamani, a Chief of Akwamu. It is not certain how he was able to achieve this daring feat. It appears, however, that Asamani and his men were able to trick the Danes and overcome them in the Castle which they held for nearly one year. During that period he established himself as Governor, and was said to be lavish in his gun salutes! The whole incident is significant because it is the only occasion on record when a European Fort along our shores was captured, almost single handed, by an African.

The Castle was subsequently bought over by the British Government in 1850, and was held by them until we occupied it in 1957.

It was on the 18th May, 1957, shortly after independence, that it was decided to establish the Castle as the Seat of Government. This had been for a long time the seat of power and government of colonial powers. It was important, and indeed psychologically necessary that he people's government should be seen to operate from the Castle. Only in this way would the masses of the people realise that effective power was now in the hands of their own elected leaders, and that the might of the colonial ruler was no more. Six years have passed since then, and three years since we adopted the Republican Constitution.

The move from the Castle to Flagstaff House in 1959 was made in order that repairs and renovations could be carried out. It was while this work was going on that it was decided to build these new Cabinet Offices, which while being modern and contemporary in style, would harmonise with the original architecture of the Castle. And this is what you see around you here to-day.

These new buildings which we are opening to-day will therefore become the focal point in the administration of the State by providing suitable offices for the Cabinet, Ministers and other public officers. The standard of accommodation provided in these buildings is high, and comparable to the best anywhere in the world. Besides a well-equipped Cabinet Room, provision has been made for Offices, Conference Rooms, a spacious Library, and Lounges for Ministers and Visitors. A special Lounge is provided for Ambassadors, High Commissioners, Diplomats and visiting dignitaries.

Great credit goes to the Architects, Messrs. Nickson and Borys, who designed these buildings, and also to the Contractors, Ghana National Construction Corporation who built them.

I am pleased to say that the rooms and grounds of the Castle will be open all day tomorrow to members of the public who wish to inspect them from six o'clock in the morning to six o'clock in the evening. I hope that as many of you as possible will make use of this opportunity.

The Government of India has very kindly presented us with a magnificent carpet, specially manufactured for the Presidential Office in the Castle. We are most grateful for this gesture of goodwill.

We expect that all who are privileged to work in these buildings will continue to be imbued with the spirit of service and devotion to Ghana and to Africa. From now on, these Offices shall be the seat of the Government of the Republic of Ghana, and shall be known and referred to as THE CASTLE, Accra.

And now, Your Excellencies and Friends, it is a pleasant duty for me to declare the offices of the Castle formally open.

17

OPENING OF
THE UNILEVER SOAP FACTORY

Tema
August 24, 1963

I am glad of the opportunity of opening this Factory to-day. It is one more proof of our ability to attract to our country, under conditions of independence, investment of a type which we never had before. This fine and efficient Factory is not the result of charity from one of the more developed countries of the world. It has been built—let us be frank—by one of the most hard-headed business combines operating in Africa today. They have built it because they believe that their investment will be safe in Ghana and that they will make a fair profit from their enterprise.

It is the skill and know-how of Lever Brothers which is responsible for the construction of this valuable asset to our economy; but, however great their financial resources, however extensive their technical experience, this Factory would never have been built but for the political skill and sagacity of the ordinary people of Ghana. Let us never forget that it was they, and they alone, who secured our independence and thus created the basic conditions which made possible a commercial investment, of the magnitude of that which has been responsible in this enterprise.

It is, however, not only the favourable climate for investment, created by the Government of Ghana, which has resulted in industrial development such as this soap factory now before us. The educational policy inaugurated by the Convention People's Party in 1951, when for the first time we had a limited degree of control over our own affairs, is now bearing fruit. We have a growing number of skilled technicians and in some fields the technical ability of our workers can to-day compare favourably with that of any country in the world. This is an important factor in encouraging foreign investment. After all, it is the labour efficiency of each and everyone of us, skilled or unskilled, which will be the decisive factor in our development. The ability of the Ghanaian citizen must reveal itself in work. Love and respect for work and concern for state and co-operative property must be the cornerstone and backbone of our Ghanaian society. Education and labour must go hand in hand. To the Ghanaian, therefore, work must not only be an obligation, it must be also a civic duty. "By the sweat of thy brow thou shalt eat bread"—so goes the biblical saying.

In order to pay a tribute to the importance of labour in the development of Ghana, the Government has decided to institute a special order to be known as the "Order of the Black Star of Labour." This honour, the details of which will shortly be announced, will rank among the highest honours of the State. It would be unfair, however, to restrict those eligible for this honour to persons who have had the good fortune in the past of obtaining a technical or professional education. All workers, whether they are school teachers or street sweepers, crane drivers or doctors, farmers or fishermen, will be equally considered for recommendation. It is immaterial whether they are engaged in Government service or private enterprise, or whether they are of managerial, supervisory or operative status. The Order will be awarded for really outstanding work in any field and will entitle the winner to be described as "the outstanding worker of the year." Let us hope that one of you here employed in this soap factory will be among the first to win this high distinction. And I say this with genuine feeling, for I shall never forget my own experience as the lowest paid labourer in a soap factory, nor my disillusionment when I discovered that soap—particularly at the low level where I came in contact with it does—not always smell so sweet and fresh!

I am pleased to open this Factory because I believe that the very fact that it has been built in an independent African State is proof of a new relationship with foreign investors which has been established through the liberation of a great part of our Continent.

The Unilever Group have a long history of association with Africa. They began their operations in our part of the world—and again let me be frank—because they wished for a cheap source of raw material for soap, which they manufactured in Europe and sold back to, among others, those very countries from which they had so cheaply exported the raw material, at a price which showed a handsome margin of profit. Starting from this comparatively modest beginning with soap, Lever Brothers have gradually accumulated the capital which has, in our own day, produced a financial giant. The first Lord Leverhulme's endeavours to establish African plantations to provide raw materials for the European industrial enterprises of Lever Brothers led them to acquire the Niger Company. In the first period of colonial exploitation this Niger Company had been granted a Charter by Britain entitling it to have dominion over the then British West African territories. Therefore, when Lever Brothers bought the Niger Company they inherited a commercial organisation which had established a predominant economic position and acquired a certain political attitude of mind because it had been, during the first fourteen years of its existence, the actual ruler of a large part of West Africa. Such was our first experience of what developments are possible from a well-run soap industry. Subsequent amalgamations with other trading concerns in the end resulted in the creation of one of Lever Brothers' most important subsidiaries, the United Africa Company. The activities of this Company had an important influence both on the economic and the political conditions in Ghana under colonial rule. Like all European trading companies, the United Africa Company began with the belief that profit could only be made from a Colony by exporting raw material from the territory and importing manufactured goods into it. Their investments were therefore used to create an efficient commercial machine devoted to wholesale and retail trading and to the purchase of cocoa, which had taken the place of the palm oil, which had originally attracted Lever Brothers to Ghana. The trowing capital of the Company was used to provide the shipping and the handling facilities, together with the credit financing necessary to sustain this colonial pattern of import and export trade. Subconsciously, therefore, the United Africa Company became itself a part of that colonial system which condemned Africa to be an exporter of cheap priced cash crops and mineral ores and the importer of expensive manufactured goods. When the people of Ghana began to revolt against colonial conditions the United Africa Company thus found themselves involved, from the very nature of their business, on the side of the colonialists. The cocoa hold-up of 1937 and the boycott of imported goods of 1948 are two examples of how this involvement with colonialism adversely affected the business prospects of those expatriate firms which, up till then, had accepted without question the theory that the only possible pattern of trade and investment was the colonial one.

It is a credit to the United Africa Company that is was able to read the writing on the wall.

This Factory which I am opening to-day is by no means the first industry established in Ghana by Lever Brothers, or its subsidiary, the United Africa Company. As independence approached, the Lever Brothers Group of Companies came to realise that profit was more likely, and investment safer, if they abandoned the old colonial ideas of trade and devoted their capital to productive industry.

Ladies and Gentlemen: If I comment on this change today, it is because soap is so symbolic. It was with soap that it all began. Now the wheel has turned the full circle and Lever Brothers, who originally came to Ghana for the raw material, are to-day manufacturing here the finished product.

This particular example of productive investment underlines the change which independence has brought. It also illustrates, unfortunately, how the advantages of independence are limited by the, absence of African Unity. The fact that this Factory is not three or four times its present size is not because Lever Brothers could not afford to build a larger Factory. It is because our disunity means that f there is an insufficiently large market for its products. Many African States still impose customs duties and import restrictions originally designed to limit the trade of the colony in the interest of the manufacturing industries of the Imperial power. The political links may have been broken, but too often on the African Continent we are still, bound by the chains of a colonial economic system. In colonial days the Imperial powers had no interest in developing trade between each other's colonies and therefore our communication system—our roads and our railways—lead outwards to our ports and thence to Europe, instead of inwards and spanning our Continent. It is not only our system of tariffs that prevents us trading with one another; it is also the absence of lines of communication along which trade can flow.

In consequence, if we have factories at all, we can only have small ones; and the price of our manufactured goods is far higher, than it need be if there was a larger market. Not only do we surfer from this: the foreign investor suffers equally. He is denied the profit which can only be made from large-scale industry and, however willing he may be to invest, his investment is limited by the smallness of the market.

Ladies and Gentlemen: I should like to say this to the expatriate business community. Your vested interest in African unity is as great as that of any African today.

It is, however, necessary to understand what is meant by African Unity. It would be of no value to the foreign investor if we merely constructed intercontinental roads and railways and abolished customs duties between African States unless we at the same time established overall economic planning. Otherwise each African State would soon find itself engaged in a cut-throat competition with its neighbour. Obviously the only sensible plan is to decide which state shall concentrate upon which industry, and upon which industrial products, uniform revenue taxes shall be imposed. These decisions can only be made by an all African political Government that is to say, a Union Government of Africa which has overall powers of economic planning and taxation. Indeed, by every day that we delay our unity, we are making ourselves poorer, and the profits of the investor diminishing. By setting up small industrial units in each State, each producing the same product, we are establishing an entirely uneconomic pattern of industrialisation which, in fact, is unlikely ever to enable us completely to escape from a colonial economic position. The longer we delay African unity, the more difficult it will be to rationalise our industrial pattern when we achieve it. The foreign investor, therefore, has an equal interest with African consumer in the speediest possible attainment of African unity.

The foreign investor has a further interest in common with the people of Africa. His profit is directly proportional to their prosperity. However large the market area, no product can be sold unless the people of that area are wealthy enough to buy it. If the economy of any African State gets out of hand, if, for example there is a balance of payments crisis, then not only will the investor be unable to export his earnings but the market on which he depend for the sale of his product will be endangered.

Ladies and Gentlemen: Whatever systems may be possible in other parts of the world, the situation on the African Continent is such that I believe the economy can only be kept in balance and economic progress assured by a socialist planning and policy.

The economy of all African States is at the mercy of changes in the terms of trade. Experience has shown that in Ghana we can increase the volume of our exports and decrease the volume of our imports and yet, owing to a change in the terms of trade, our exports are worth less and imports cost more than they did before. It is only by a State monopoly of the export of cocoa and of other cash crops that we can hope to control this tendency by which exports from less developed countries tend always to fall in value. An uncontrolled right to import would soon exhaust our reserves of foreign currency and if we are to restrict imports we must do it in accordance with an overall plan which encourages productive development and which prevents the necessarily limited quantity of imports being wasted on unproductive use.

The traditional economic organisation of African society severely limits the capital any individual can amass. Under our conditions, if capital is to be supplied it must be supplied by the State from the produce of public saving. This does not of course mean that there is no place for private investment in the Ghanaian system. On the contrary, we regard private investment originating from both outside and inside the country as an important factor in our development. It does mean, however, that private investment should be channelled into those industries which will fit our plans for development.

The history of colonial Africa is a lesson we must all take to heart. It is an experience worth always remembering. When external capital is merely applied for the purpose of obtaining a quick profit it more often impoverishes rather than enriches the country in which it is invested. For example, the extraction and exportation of mineral ores through the use of imported machinery and by the employment of low paid labour is of no material benefit to the people of the country concerned. Ultimately the mineral resources of the colonial country are exhausted and the imported machinery is moved elsewhere, or scrapped. The labour that was employed, having been paid only a subsistence wage, will have accumulated no savings. Thus nothing remains upon which future development can be based. This was one of the commonest types of capital investment in colonial Africa and it is still to be found, unfortunately, in some independent African States. It is a type of investment we are not prepared to tolerate and this was one of the reasons for the enactment of the Capital Investments Act.

This Act, which would have been unthinkable in colonial times, is in itself a proof of the changed relationship between foreign investors and the Government of Ghana. While it gives substantial advantages to those who invest in Ghana, it also imposes important obligations. Foreign investors must to-day fit their investment to suit the overall plan for the development of our economy. They must maintain a high level of employment and impart technical skill to the Ghanaians whom they employ, a thing which unhappily by no means always happened in the past. The Act is in no way contrary to our overall plan for the socialist development of the country. Indeed, it is a necessary part of it. In colonial days productive investment by foreign investors was prevented in many direct and indirect ways and we therefore entered upon independence with a very low level of industrialisation. We have now to use every means in our power to reverse this position, and this Act is one of them.

Some people think the Capital Investment Act is in contradiction with our socialist aims and ideas. This is not true. However, we are realists and therefore we welcome any foreign investor who is prepared to respond to the socialist conditions in an independent Ghana.

It is because this Soap Factory represents a response to these new conditions that I am happy to open it to-day. It was their interest in soap that first brought Lever Brothers to our shores. I hope their undertaking of its manufacture in our country will increase their interest in investment generally in Ghana. After all, if one compares the weather enjoyed in Ghana with that enjoyed in Britain, there can be no doubt in which country the Lever Brothers' capital "Port Sunlight" ought to be situated!

I wish once again to congratulate Lever Brothers for establishing this Factory and for the other substantial investments which they have made in productive enterprises in Ghana.

And now Ladies and Gentlemen, I have great pleasure in declaring this factory open.

18

TRIBUTE TO
DR. W. E. B. DU BOIS

Accra
August 29, 1963

We mourn the death of Dr. William Edward Burghardt Du Bois, a great son of Africa.

Dr. Du Bois, in a long life-span of 96 years, achieved distinction as a poet, historian and sociologist. He was an undaunted fighter for the emancipation of colonial and oppressed people, and pursued this objective throughout his life.

The fields of literature and science were enriched by his profound and searching scholarship, a brilliant literary talent, and a keen and penetrating mind. The seenetial quality of Dr. Du Bois' life and achievement can be summed up in a single phrase: intellectual honesty and integrity.

Dr. Du Bois was a distinguished figure in the pioneering days of the Pan African Movement in the Western World. He was the Secretary of the First Pan African Congress held in London in 1900. In 1919 he organised another Pan African Congress in Paris which coincided with the Paris Peace Conference. When George Padmore and I organised the Fifth Pan African Congress in 1945 at Manchester, we invited Dr. Du Bois, then already 78 years of age, to chair that Congress. I knew him in the United States and even spoke on the same platform with him. It was however at this Conference in Manchester that I was drawn closely to him. Since then he has been personally a real friend and father to me.

Dr. Du Bois was a life-long fighter against all forms of racial inequality, discrimination and injustice. He helped to establish the National Association for the Advancement of Coloured People, and was the first editor of its fighting organ *The Crisis*. Concerning the struggle for the improvement of the status of the Negro in America, he once said:

"We will not be satisfied to take one jot or little less than our full manhood rights. We claim for ourselves every single right that belongs to a free-born American, political, civil and social; and until we get these fights we will never cease to protest and assail the ears of America. The battle we wage is not for ourselves alone, but all true Americans."

It was the late George Padmore who described Dr. Du Bois as the greatest scholar the Negro race has produced, and one who always upheld the right of Africans to govern themselves.

I asked Dr. Du Bois to come to Ghana to pass the evening of his life with us and also to spend his remaining years in compiling an *Encyclopaedia Africana*, a project which is part of his whole intellectual life. We mourn his death. May he live in our memory not only as a distinguished scholar, but as a great African Patriot. Dr. Du Bois is a phenomenon. May he rest in peace.

19

NATIONAL FOUNDER'S DAY

1963

I share your feelings to-day as you assemble to celebrate our National Founder's Day.

To the nation, this is an important occasion. It is a day on which we all reflect on our duty to the nation, on the cultivation of those virtues which will promote the well being of us all, and our aspirations and hopes for the future. It is fitting therefore that we should remind ourselves of the great responsibilities we owe to our country.

You must be sure to take full advantage of the facilities available to you now, and so equip yourselves that you may be able, in future, to make your contribution to the progress of the land that gave you birth. In your daily lives it should be your constant endeavour to cultivate those attributes of excellence and perfection which are the characteristics of a good citizen. You must be disciplined and hard working, responsible and reliable and dedicated to the best and highest qualities of man.

You can assist in the reconstruction of Ghana by constant devotion to your work, and by showing due respect to all those placed in authority over you. Our society has no place for laziness or irresponsibility. Our aim is to create a society in which the good things of life will be available to all who freely and diligently contribute to the national effort. This will be your heritage and your challenge.

May the celebrations to-day make you more conscious than ever of your obligations and the duty you owe to Ghana—the land of our birth.

I wish you all a happy and successful National Founder's Day.

20

GHANA MILITARY ACADEMY PASSING-OUT PARADE

Teshie, Accra
September 14, 1963

It is a great pleasure for me to be with you this afternoon at this parade of cadets from the Military Academy.

For you who are passing out to-day this ceremony is an important event. It marks a significant occasion which must be the proudest moment of your life. The command of a platoon which you will shortly be privileged to hold is one of the most exacting and responsible duties in the life of an officer. It is the beginning of an interesting but difficult career in which it will be your constant duty to demonstrate selfless devotion and loyalty to your Government and country.

The Presidential commission which you will receive from me is a symbol of the trust and responsibility which will be placed upon you. I have every confidence that you will carry out your duties in such a way as to bring credit not only to yourselves but to our Army and to Ghana.

The life of a soldier is not easy. It demands toughness and a keen sense of duty and discipline. Those who join the Armed Forces, therefore, must not do so for reasons of personal advancement, comfort or self-interest. These things have no place in our Armed Forces.

Although we in Ghana, like the rest of the world, must maintain Armed Forces for self-defence, it is the hope of mankind, which we share, that one day total and complete disarmament will be achieved. When that day comes the Armies of the world will really turn their swords into ploughshares, and the battlegrounds of the soldier will become the battlements and highways dedicated to progress, reconstruction, world advancement and the permanent removal of all causes of war.

I am happy to note that the Ghana Armed Forces are already participating actively through relief work and by other means in the development of Ghana. The assistance which the Armed Forces are giving, at the present time, to our kinsmen of the Northern and Upper Regions shows how the skill and experience of the Armed services can be brought to bear in our national effort and reconstruction.

It is only four years ago since I caused to be established the Ghana Military Academy. Within this short space of time this institution has shown commendable signs of progress. I have been impressed by the rapid expansion and high standards achieved during this period. I should like therefore to congratulate all the members of staff under whose leadership and guidance the Military Academy has become the first-rate institution which it is to-day.

Let me stress again the importance of discipline which is the basis on which the efficiency of the Armed Forces is built. Self-discipline is the key to the life of the Army as it is of the nation. To achieve the confidence and trust of the men under your command and to assist and guide them effectively, you yourselves must set an example of a disciplined life. It is only through this personal example that you can command spontaneous respect among your men.

As you receive your Commissions to-day, you will come under the constant and watchful eyes not only of your men, but also of those of us who are your superior officers.

You must never forget that to be a good soldier is to be a good citizen, and to be a good citizen is to be a good soldier. It is therefore important that you should identify yourselves closely with the affairs and policies of the Government and the aspirations of our Party and the people. I am glad to learn in this connection that a Bureau of Current Affairs has been formed in the Army in order to keep the officers and other ranks fully informed of what the Party and the Government are doing for the people of Ghana and Africa and in world affairs.

I hope that in due course we shall be able to establish here in Ghana a Higher Military Academy for the training of superior Military Officers, capable of serving the needs of a continental government of Africa.

I am happy that some of you have volunteered for the next gliding course which begins in Afienya shortly. You can be sure that you have a great experience ahead of you. Your knowledge of gliding will promote the qualities of self-control, courage and calmness which you have already developed. I trust that more of you will take up this exciting sport.

And now, I would like, once again, to congratulate you who are passing out to-day. Particular mention must be made of SENIOR UNDER OFFICER R. DZOGBENUKU who has won the coveted Sword of Honour, and also of Officer Cadet W. A. ODJIDJA for achieving the highest academic grading on the course.

I wish you all the best of luck.

SESSIONAL REVIEW OF THE THIRD SESSION OF THE FIRST PARLIAMENT OF THE REPUBLIC OF GHANA

Since I addressed you in September last year, a major and decisive step has been taken towards the realisation of our cherished dream of African Unity. By the signing of the Charter of the Organisation of African Unity at Addis Ababa last May, we are set directly on a course leading to a continental union of Africa. There is now concerted action by the countries of Africa for the realisation of this common objective. We shall continue to work relentlessly until we reach this goal.

Already some of the Commissions set up by the Charter of the Organisation of African Unity, have started work in earnest. The Provisional Commission has already met in Addis Ababa where it has done useful work of co-ordination. Already the Co-ordinating Committee, known as the Committee of Nine, has met in Dar-es-Salaam to plan and organise the Liberation Front. The effect of the determination of all Heads of African States to liquidate colonialism in Africa is being felt in certain quarters. Dr. Salazar of Portugal, shaken by our joint determination, has been making statements which can only be the outcome of moral discomfiture, guilt and fear. More African States than ever have placed an embargo on South African goods, and have banned South African ships and planes from their countries. In sympathy with the principles of African Unity, the Security Council of the United Nations has called on all States to cease forthwith the sale and shipment of arms and ammunition of all types and of military equipment to South Africa. In Geneva, at the recent conference of the International Labour Organisation (ILO), all the African delegates spoke with one voice and acted in the true spirit of African Unity.

Within the last two months, there have been other manifestations of true spirit of African Unity in the visits that have been made to

Accra by a few Leaders of African States. President Grunitsky of Togo has twice visited Ghana recently. President Ben Bella of Algeria, one of the great heroes of the Algeria revolution has been here. Mr. Odinga and Mr. Koinarge, Ministers in the Government of Kenya, were with us a few weeks ago. The last but not the least of the visitors to Ghana in recent times was our friend and redoubtable freedom fighter, Dr. Kamuzu Hastings Banda. In their rapid succession to one another these visits more than anything else serve to bring us closer together and create strong bonds of intimacy so necessary in our concerted endeavour to free Africa of all colonialist and neo-colonialist forces, and to carve out a continental form of government.

We are confident that upon these foundations, a super-structure of complete Continental, Political Union of Africa will be achieved. It is now that we have come to real grips with the problems that have confronted us in our struggle for African Unity and African Freedom. There is no turning back. Colonialist auld neo-colonialist intrigues, manoeuvres and obstructions must be subdued. In these exciting and challenging times, it is the duty of every Ghanaian, of every African, to contribute his maximum towards our goal of Unity and total liberation of Africa. Let it be the proudest hope of us all to be of some service in this noble and great endeavour.

As we all know, the British Government has now given its blessing to the dismemberment and dissolution of the Central African Federation. Naturally, Nyasaland and Northern Rhodesia, who now enjoy Internal Self-government, have not hesitated to take advantage of this constitutional advance which by their organised strength they have forced Britain to concede. Already the African delegates at the United Nations have taken energetic action and a united stand on the Southern Rhodesia question and the Organisation of African Unity is determined to see the question solved in the true spirit of African nationalism. The mid-20th century anachronism of colonialism and minority-settler domination in Africa most and will be brought to an end at all events.

The Ghana Government recently submitted to the Security Council a memorandum on the issue of Southern Rhodesia. At the meeting of the Council the voice of Africa was united and strong.

Britain was forced to use the veto, the last weapon in her hand and a clumsy substitute for convincing arguments at the world forum. But, our fellow freedom fighters will remain confident in the knowledge that the crumbling walls of the Federation are falling fast on the shoulders of racialist adventurers. The wheels of freedom are turning faster. Independence for our brothers of Zimbabwe is in sight.

Since I addressed you on the Second of October, 1962, Uganda has become a Sovereign State, and Ghana has already established a Diplomatic Mission there. Before the end of this year Kenya and Zanzibar will also attain their independence and become Sovereign, States. The Gambia and Nyasaland are moving fast to nationhood. Gradually, but surely, more and more African States will shake off their colonial bondage, despite the intransigence of colonial powers and their ruthless manoeuvres to thwart and obstruct the legitimate aspirations of millions struggling to be free.

On 1st October, that is a few days hence, we shall hail the founding of Nigeria as a Federal Republic. You will recall that the First October this year will be the third Anniversary of Nigeria's Independence. We in Ghana will certainly rejoice with our brothers in Nigeria on this great occasion of the birth of the Republic of Nigeria.

Ghana and Togo have agreed to exchange Diplomatic Missions and already Ghana has established a Mission in Lome. This augurs well for our future relations. This is in furtherance of the policy of the Ghana Government to set up Missions in all Independent African Countries. We have made good progress in this respect and hope to be able to fulfil this policy completely in the very near future.

During the year under review, Ghana played a significant role in the pursuit of world peace and security. We played an important part in the effort to bring about a peaceful settlement of the Sino-Indian border dispute. At the invitation of the Prime Minister of Ceylon, Mrs. Bandranike, Ghana and five other Afro-Asian non-aligned countries met in Colombo in the second week of December, 1962 and drew up proposals designed to create the atmosphere for peaceful and direct negotiations between India and China. It is gratifying to recall that it was largely through this action of the Colombo Powers that a situation which might easily have erupted into war was brought at least under temporary control. Ghana will, in concert with her sister Afro-Asian countries that met in Colombo, continue in her conciliatory efforts until there is a complete settlement of the Sino-Indian border dispute through peaceful negotiations.

In an attempt to strengthen the unity and solidarity of the Afro-Asian countries, Ghana has urged the solution, by peaceful negotiations, of the Kashmir problem between India and Pakistan. For the solution of the Arab-Israeli problem Ghana has suggested that the approach to the Middle East question in general should be governed by two principles, namely:-

(i) The need to keep power-bloc conflicts out of the Middle East, and

(ii) The recognition of the independence and territorial integrity of each Middle East State by all the other States in the area.

The problem of disarmament still remains with us. As I remarked in a statement at the United Nations in 1960, the cause of disarmament has suffered possibly because it is looked upon in a negative way. This negative approach arose from the lack of faith on both sides. Today, the world can rejoice that that lost faith is in the process of being rediscovered. Despite the unfavourable and cynical reaction of certain Powers to it, the tripartite nuclear Test Ban Treaty recently concluded in Moscow is a step in the right direction. The conclusion of the Treaty has, to say the least, relieved the hopes of mankind for the survival of civilisation and unleashed new forces of thinking and planning for peace. Ghana has become a party to the Treaty in the hope that it will lead to general and complete disarmament at an early date.

I should like to state, in conclusion of this account of our international relations, that during the year under review, Ghana signed 26 Agreements and Protocols with Foreign countries including the United States of America, the Soviet Union, and United Arab Republic, Israel, China, Rumania, West Germany, Japan and the Niger Republic. The Agreements cover Trade and Payments, Technical Co-operation, Reciprocal Air Services, Maritime Transport Relations and Cultural Exchanges. Besides these, the implementation of the

Agreements signed with various countries in 1961 proceeded apace.

It is gratifying to observe that our Foreign Policy of Positive Neutralism, pursuit of world peace and above all African Unity and our uncompromising stand against colonialism, neo-colonialism and imperialism has been vigorously pursued during the session, and with much success.

Ghana maintains continued interest in the promotion of inter-African Trade. Such an interest has not been heightened by the recent Addis Ababa Conference of Heads of State.

Though Trade is generally appraised in the context of the material gains it brings to the participating countries, there are other gains such as bonds of friendship and understanding which it offers imperceptibly between trading countries. These imperceptible bonds become transformed into concrete ties which constitute a unifying force when trade is conducted in terms of a Common Market.

While sparing no effort in our work on the African Common Market, everything is being done to increase the country's export earnings. One of the best methods of inviting attention to the availability of commodities is by participation in trade fairs. Ghana has participated in trade fairs in Czechoslovakia, Yugoslavia, Poland, U.S.S.R. and Nigeria. Also at the invitation of the Government of German Democratic Republic and Italy, official Ghanaian delegations visited the Leipzig Fair and the Milan International Trade Fair. In these fairs large volumes of business were transacted and statistics show that there is an expansion in our trade with the countries visited.

Arrangements for organising an International Trade Fair in Ghana are well in hand. Advance notices have already been given to the various governments of the World's trading nations.

During the year two high-powered Trade Missions from Pakistan and Hungary visited the country with the main object of promoting trade and investments to our mutual advantage. These held useful talks with interested parties in Government and in private business.

In the field of industrialisation, Ghana continued to make a steady progress. Projects completed during the year included the Jute Bag Factory at Kumasi, the Oil Refinery at Tema and five small vegetable oil mills at Atebubu, Tamale, Bawku, Asesewa and Denu. Construction work on the following projects were started: two cocoa processing factories at Tema and Takoradi, a Textile Printing Works, a Steel Works Plant at Tema, a Meat Processing Factory at Bolgatanga, and a Packing Plant at Takoradi. It is expected that all of these projects will go into production next year.

It is the aim of the Government that as far as possible, industries should be established in the rural areas to stimulate economic activity in those areas, carry work to the people, and arrest the steady drift of the population into the cities and big towns, from the countryside. In pursuit of that objective, a number of smallscale industries were started and these are nearing completion. These consist of Bamboo Factories at Axim, Manso-Amenfi, and Assin Foso; Coir Processing Factories at Half Assini, Saltpond and Denu; a Garment Factory at Suhum; and Ratten Factories at Enyiresi, Asamankese, Nkawkaw, Bobikuma, Oppon Valley and Asanwinso. It is the declared aim of the Government to encourage and support small-scale and cottage industries of all kinds not only to create more employment opportunities but also to enhance the foreign-exchange earning potential of such industries.

Private investors continue to play an active role in the industrial development of the country. Among factories that have sprung up in this sector were those for the manufacture of perfumes, detergents and insecticides, cotton fabrics, travel bags, spring interior mattresses, raincoats, plastic goods, incense and car batteries. At Tema I recently performed the official opening of a large soap factory which will in due course provide all our requirements of soap.

One of the major legislations passed during the year was the Capital Investments Act which consolidates all the measures taken to stimulate activity in the private sector and to define the nature of concessions that may be granted for investments so made. I am happy to say that the effect of this Act has been most encouraging and many private investors continue to flock in with proposals to establish business in Ghana.

Our Agricultural policy is to increase our food production, to improve the nutrition of our increasing population and also to provide the raw materials for domestic industries and exports. The main emphasis has been on mechanisation and training. Already several thousands of farm machinery are being utilised, and hundreds of Ghanaian students have gone abroad on courses of specialised training in Agriculture and fishing operations.

On the production front, the State Farms Corporation and the Agricultural Wing of the Workers Brigade have continued to make very big strides in the establishment of large-scale farms. To date, a total of 105 State Farms and 34 Brigade Farms have been established in all the Regions with well over 20,000 acres crippled with maize, guinea-corn, rice, vegetables, tobacco and cotton. The Workers Brigade also have over 8,000 acres under cultivation. 15,000 acres have in addition been planted with rubber, cola, citrus, banana, oil palm and coconut. Similarly the various co-operative and individual farmers who form the largest portion of the farming community have continued to make a very satisfactory impact on agricultural production. In the Western Region for example well over 5,000 acres have been put under rubber production by co-operative effort. During the year, Ghana produced over 450,000 tons of cocoa, our principal revenue earner. Ninety-nine point nine per cent of this large output was classified as grade one. This testifies to the hard work and efficiency of our farmers. A favourable market overseas has been found for coffee with the selling price of pound G200 per ton. Our coffee export this year has risen to 1,900 tons.

The problem of water for the savannah areas of the country which are largely suitable for mechanized farming has been tackled with the utmost vigour.

A total of 263 Dams have so far been built for irrigation of nearly 10,000 acres of land for sugar and rice production in the lower Volta Plain, near Akuse.

Two trawlers, each with a capacity of 240 tons have been procured and orders have been placed for 36 more vessels.

Over 600 N'dama cattle have been imported from Guinea and Mali and these are being bred and multiplied. Another 500 are expected shortly.

The programme of Internal Food Distribution is being pursued realistically. Concrete silos and refrigeration plants are being installed in all major food distributing centres.

My Government's decision to supply free text-books to all approved Primary, Middle and Secondary Schools has been implemented. Already, very large stocks of text-books have been delivered for distribution to all schools throughout the eight Regions of Ghana.

Our fee-free education programme continues to gather momentum. A total of 1,412 Primary and 239 Middle Schools were opened during the period under review—1962-63.

Preliminary work has been completed for introducing effective science teaching into Middle Schools. Briefing Courses have been organised for a number of certificated teachers in Science and Mathematics.

The year saw an increase in the number of Secondary Schools from 68 to 74. Enrollment in these schools leapt by 5,000 to 23,000. Sixth Form enrollment is being stepped up to 1,500 this very month. Syllabuses have been re-cast in conformity with out decision to reduce the secondary school course from five to four years.

Our teacher training programme is being re-vitalized.

Advanced courses have been provided for training technicians and engineers.

The Institute of Public Education has vastly expanded its work of providing education to the workers of Ghana. By December, 1962, it had increased it enrollment to well over 10,000.

An institute has been established for degree courses in statistics. The University College of Cape Coast has been established to provide Diploma and degree courses for work in secondary schools and teacher-training colleges.

The combined enrollment of the University of Ghana and the Kwame Nkrumah University of Science and Technology has increased to 2,000. Nearly 10 per cent of these are students from other African States of Nigeria, Nyasaland, Kenya, Tanganyika,

Uganda as well as from the United States of America, the United Kingdom and Germany.

Ghana provided the venue for the first International Congress of Africanists held on African soil.

Among scholars who have participated in the work of our universities are those from Ouagadougou, California, Cambridge, Oxford, Harvard, Ibadan and London School of Economics.

The research institutes of the Ghana Academy of Sciences have become international centres where scientists from many nations work together in peace and harmony.

The work of producing an Encyclopaedia Africana has gone forward and the Secretariat charged with this assignment has received considerable support from scholars and institutions of learning in other parts of Africa and is now organising regional committees to assist in this important intellectual and cultural undertaking.

The Government has forged ahead in its determination to make medical services available to all sections of the nation and remarkable strides have been made in the provision of health services at both rural and urban levels. Existing hospitals are being modernized and extended to reduce congestion in them and a number of health centres have been built. The various training programmes in health services have been considerably revised with a view of producing more doctors, nurses and paramedical staff to man the various health institutions in the country. A pilot scheme has been instituted the results of which will be utilized for medical and dental examination of all school children. Our plans for the construction of a medical school and a teaching hospital have made good progress. Already the pioneer students of the Medical Schools have just completed their first year training.

The provision of the infrastructure for Ghana's industrial and agricultural revolution has been undertaken with vigour. A tremendous amount of constructional work has been undertaken. For example the flood water of Accra have been brought under control. Road works throughout the country have been accelerated and much resealing and resurfacing works have been undertaken.

In co-operation with a United Nations Regional Planning Mission a national physical development plan has been drawn up to provide the geographical and locational framework for our development projects and for the economic and social reconstruction of the country.

Our Community Development Programme continues to gain in strength and to offer reliable means of building up self-confidence in our people. Much progress has been stimulated especially in rural areas. This year over 1,000 self-help projects have been completed. Over 3,000 Village Development Committees have been established. Over 2,500 Co-operative Societies, including industrial and agricultural co-operatives, have been registered.

We have intensified our efforts to provide adequate supplies of good drinking water for the masses of the people in all the Regions of the country.

Throughout the year we have continued to maintain a contingent of the Ghana Armed Forces in the Congo under the United Nations Command. Our troops continue to distinguish themselves in their service in the Congo and have earned a good name for the Ghana Armed Forces. Their efforts in helping to bring trouble-torn Congo to peaceful ways are most commendable.

Ghana is a peace-loving country. Our Armed Forces are therefore being rapidly reconditioned to the peaceful task of reconstruction along with their task of safe-guarding our hard-won independence.

The Volta River Project represents Ghana's main hope for a rapid industrial and agricultural revolution. Members of the House no less than myself and our fellow citizens of Ghana are therefore naturally interested in the smooth operation of the plans set out in this giant Project. The annual report of the Volta River Authority has already been laid before you.

I am glad to inform the House that work on all phases of the Project is proceeding according to schedule. 37 percent of the total work on the Project has been completed to date. It is confidently expected that the Dam will be completed on schedule; and the Volta Hydro will begin to generate and supply electric power in late 1965.

The settlement work has been greatly accelerated. About 2,000 houses have already been completed and 4,000 acres of new farm land cleared for these settlements.

I am happy to state that thanks to the principle of open international competitive tendering followed in the award of contracts and the diligence and care exercised by Government, the total cost of the project is now estimated at 56.2 million Ghanaian pounds as against the original estimate of 70 million Ghanaian pounds.

Nearly 3,300 personnel are now engaged on the construction and resettlement activities. Of these, about 3,000 are Ghanaians.

The Volta Dam and the Volta Lake offer vast potentialities for multi-purpose development in diverse fields—in industry, irrigated agriculture, fisheries and river navigation.

I said in my message during the last Session that a visit to Akosombo is both a rewarding and enlightening experience. A visitor to the dam site in September, 1963 is impressed not only by the transformation of the whole scene but he witnesses vivid signs of the cherished dream of generations—the Volta Dam taking concrete shape before his eyes. The rushing waters of the Volta river have been held in check by the Dam gradually rising from month to month; a large amount of materials and equipment for the Intake and the Power House are being rapidly assembled on the ground; a new township, which may well be the location of new industries greets the visitor and he returns from such a visit with a growing hope and abiding confidence that the large financial investment in the Project should not only prove productive but the Volta lake and the Volta dam would prove the most effective instrument of strengthening the foundations of our economy and accelerating its growth to greater and higher levels.

Members of the National Assembly, I thank you for the funds which you have voted for the Public Services during the period under review.

TENTH ANNIVERSARY OF THE UNITED GHANA FARMERS' COUNCIL CO-OPERATIVES

September 26, 1963

I am glad to be here with you to celebrate the Tenth Anniversary of the United Ghana Farmers Council Co-operatives. I wish to congratulate you for your contribution towards the progress and development of Ghana.

The United Ghana Farmers Council Co-operatives is one of the vigorous arms of our Party. It was established by the peasant farmers of Ghana to sustain their collective efforts and to mobilise their energies and resources in the national interest.

It is fitting that at a time like this we should recall some of the outstanding achievements of the United Ghana Farmers Council Co-operatives. In 1954 when the Convention People's Party sought to create a stable price for cocoa by pegging the price at 72s per load, the Government's action was widely misinterpreted to the farmers by the cocoa and budget politicians. These detractors sought to destroy the confidence which you, our farmers, had in the Party and the Government. But you refused to listen to them, and you took upon yourselves to tour all the cocoa-growing areas to explain to the people the wisdom of the Government's decision.

Since 1954, the price of cocoa, on the world market, has shown a steady decline from 302 Ghanaian pounds per ton to the present average price of 190 Ghanaian pounds a ton. In spite of this, the Ghanaian cocoa farmer has continued to receive a steady price for his crop.

The United Ghana Farmers Council Co-operatives have demonstrated in many ways that the Party and the Government can rely on them and that they in turn can rely on the Government for the achievements of our common objectives in the field of cocoa production.

We are proud of the able and efficient manner in which your organisation was able to market the entire cocoa crop of the country, and raised the quality of the cocoa crop itself.

In order to preserve the cocoa industry, the scientists tell us that cutting out is the only remedy against the swollen shoot disease. I have therefore directed that a Committee composed of representatives of the United Ghana Farmers Council Co-operatives, trained agricultural officers and representatives of those who are responsible for the preservation of the cocoa industry be established to co-ordinate, direct and supervise the cutting out operations.

I am glad to learn also that the United Ghana Farmers Council has Co-operative Farms with a total acreage of not less than twenty-four thousand acres. In order to help you in your work, I have recently authorised the purchase of sixty trawler tractors; one hundred and twenty caterpillar tractors and nearly five hundred wheel tractors and agricultural implements which will be put at your disposal by your Council; arrangements have also been made for the establishment of a Tractor Assembling Plant in Ghana in order to increase the supply of tractors to meet the country's agricultural requirements.

We all know the difficulties created in the past by the absence of well organised food marketing arrangements. And we have now established a Food Marketing Board. The duties of this Board will be to formulate policies relating to all matters of food marketing; to fix maximum prices for all foodstuffs; to advise the Agricultural Production units regarding distribution of foodstuffs, and to organise the sale and storage of surplus foodstuffs for distribution when necessary to areas threatened by famine. I trust that the members of this Board will understand and discharge their responsibilities in the best interest of the nation.

Let me now mention the Future Farmers who are playing such an important part in the agricultural crusade. I vividly recall my visit recently to the George Padmore Settlement Farm at Oyarifa. The enthusiasm and spirit of sacrifice among the Future Farmers there which I saw filled me with great hope for the future of Ghana's agriculture. I can assure you that this Organisation of Future Farmers will receive from me every encouragement.

The name Future Farmers does not really do justice to this galant band of young farmers. They are already, and in fact, actively engaged in farm production, and I see no reason why they should continue to call themselves Future Farmers. They are participating fully in the agricultural Revolution of to-day. I would suggest therefore that instead of calling themselves Future Farmers they should adopt a name befitting their role. As I see it, they deserve truly to be called the Young Farmers League. With the proper co-ordination of activity between the United Ghana Farmers Council Co-operatives, and the State Farms Organisation, the Young Farmers League and the peasant farmers, I am sure that our whole agricultural effort will produce maximum results.

Every effort should be made to increase the production of those food crops that can best thrive in Ghana. Meat, fish and egg production must be increased to meet our protein requirements. Commodities such as cereals and vegetables are required in ever-increasing quantities to meet our people's basic requirements. It is economically suicidal that we should continue to import foodstuffs such as rice, corn and oranges which we can grow here with ease. This is the task and the challenge for you and the United Ghana Farmers Council Co-operatives.

Ghana has embarked on a policy of industrialisation and already we see many factories and industrial development projects throughout the country. This development, however, must be supported by increasing productivity in agriculture. In other words our plans for industrialisation depend to a large extent on the vigour and the productivity of our farming operations.

It is in this spirit that I ask you all to dedicate yourselves in the service of Ghana. Let us remember that hard work and efficiency should form the basis for your organisation. Farmers of Ghana, this is not the time for mere talk and fruitless discussion. This is the time for action. I ask each and everyone of you to be steadfast behind us in the tasks which we have set before you.

I wish you every success.

Long Live the Convention People's Party.

Long Live the United Ghana Farmers Council Co-operatives.

Long Live the Ghana Agricultural Revolution.

23

FORMAL OPENING OF THE OIL REFINERY

Tema
September 28, 1963

The opening of this oil refinery in Ghana is significant in that it marks an important stage in our investment and development programme.

Since the attainment of our political independence, there has been no doubt in our minds as to the direction in which our duty lay, namely, to develop Ghana into a modern industrial state. It is only in this way that we can survive as an independent country.

To achieve this objective, we have to rid ourselves of the economic patterns and institutions of imperialism left behind by colonialism. It was necessary to instill confidence in ourselves and to share that confidence with our people. We were convinced that we could meet and surpass all the challenges which our independence had imposed on us.

But in actual fact, we faced a greater hostility that we had dreamt of. We swung into action as one people to lay the economic foundations for a socialist Ghana. The opening of this oil refinery is a testimony of this determination.

Oil is the lifeblood of industry. It is as important for industry as water is for human existence. The politics of it is even more complicating. Without oil the wheels of industry refuse to turn. That is why the Government has decided to buttress its programme of industrialisation by the establishment of an oil refinery in Ghana.

This Oil Refinery, with its oil processing capacity of one million metric tons, and built at a cost of nearly Ghanaian pounds 8½ million, is one of the six largest refineries in Africa. As our industrial programme expands it will be possible to expand the refinery to a capacity two or three times its present size.

I can now look back to the period of long and protracted discussions which took place, leading to an agreement concluded on the 21st January, 1961, between the Government of Ghana and the AGIP MINERARIA which led to the formation of the Ghanaian-Italian Petroleum Company which has given birth to this Oil Refinery.

The Ghanaian-ltalian Petroleum Company is an inter-state enterprise of a special kind.

And here I must pay tribute to a friend. It is interesting to note that AGIP MINERARIA itself, which has given birth to Ghana-Italian Petroleum Company owes its origin and growth to the vision and foresight of a politician and entrepreneur who harnessed his commercial genius with state enterprises in his own country. This is indeed an example of how the genius and skill of patriotic citizens can be put at the disposal of the State and not for the exploitation of the many by the few.

The lamentable and untimely death of Signor Enrico Mattei in an aircrash near Milan last October, robbed Italy of one of its great captains of State Industry. It was he who formed the state-owned oil 'industry, E.N.I. out of which AGIP MINERARIA come into being. AGIP MINERARIA in its turn gave birth to the GHANAIAN-ITALIAN PETROLEUM COMPANY here in Ghana. E.N.I. prospered under Enrico Mattei's distinguished leadership, and extended its, interests widely: for example, E.N.I. controlled atomic enterprises, synthetic rubber plants, cement factories and a string of hotels.

By making Italy the largest importer of Russian oil in the West and by combining state enterprise with private capital, Signor Mattei broke the foreign oil monopolies which battered on Italy's industries and created conditions for the Italian oil industry which make it an acceptable partner for the development of our own oil industries.

The authorised share capital of the Ghanaian-Italian Petroleum Company is Three Million Four Hundred Thousand Pounds made up of ordinary shares of One Pound each. The total amount is subscribed equally by two Italian companies AGIP MINERARIA and A.N.I.C. Under the Agreement which we have signed, Ghanaian-Italian Petroleum Company will transfer to the

Government of Ghana fifty per cent of the issued capital on the eleventh anniversary of the production date (that is, the first day of the month following that in which the refinery commenced production), and the Government of Ghana will be entitled to fifty per cent share of the profits. The Government of Ghana will also appoint the Chairman of the Board of Directors and one half of the membership.

Meanwhile, Ghanaian-Italian Petroleum Company have undertaken, commencing with the production date, to pay into a Special Sinking Fund such sums as will produce, together with compound interest at settlement date, an amount equal to one-half of the cost of the Refinery; the amount paid into the Special Sinking Fund shall belong to the Government of Ghana.

This is a new form of economic and industrial relationship which Signor Mattei and I tried to evolve as another pattern of foreign investment in developing countries.

Another aspect of this Agreement is that the Ghanaian-Italian Petroleum Company will train and employ Ghanaian technical and administrative staff which eventually could take over the management. The Government of Ghana have the final say in determining the prices of the products of this Oil Refinery.

It is my Government's intention that this Refinery should become a vital part of the infrastructure for the establishment of other industries in Ghana. I have therefore directed that first among the many by-products of petroleum, immediate consideration should be given to the establishment of a fertilizer industry in Ghana. By the establishment of this fertilizer industry it will be possible to increase our present agricultural production many times over.

When I had the occasion a month ago to open another industrial enterprise, the Unilever Soap Factory here in Tema, I pointed out the need for continental planning in Africa. This Oil Refinery could have been built with an initial capacity five times its present size. But this could not be done because of our limitation in money and resources. This limitation was caused solely by the fact of our disunity in Africa which precludes planning on a continental basis. For, as long as we remain disunited and our trade remains subject to the interests of the manufacturing industries of the imperialist powers, we cannot achieve large-scale industrial development in Africa. Thus, for example, if our imports are more than our exports, and our trade balance unfavourable, and if our reserves are such that we cannot off-set our budget deficit, then we cannot stand up to the ravages and overtures of the neo-colonialist powers. Here we have another illustration of how the African States have denied themselves of the full advantages of development by the absence of continental unity and a unified economic continental planning.

I am glad to welcome to this ceremony Mr. Marcello Boldrini, the President of E.N.I., and His Excellency Mr. Giorgio Bo, Italian Minister of State Participation. You see, even in Italy there is a Minister for State Participation. I would like to express to them and to the other delegates of the Italian Government and AGIP MINERARIA, our appreciation of their efforts for the interest in helping to establish this Oil Refinery in Ghana.

The factory buildings which we all see here are of the most modern design and construction: the machinery is of the most modern in its class. Within these factory buildings, we shall be producing for the first time in Ghana liquid petroleum gas, normal gasoline, premium gasoline and diesel oil, kerosene, gas oil and fuel oil—all of which will stimulate industrial activity. These "made in Ghana" petroleum products will make for a substantial reduction in our dependence on imported sources of energy. This Refinery will help us to acquire new skills and contribute greatly to our national development.

I am sure that what we see here to-day is only the beginning of an important upsurge in our industrial programme. May this Refinery justify the confidence and the faith which our people have placed in us and in its success.

And now, Your Excellencies, Nananom, Ladies and Gentlemen, I have great pleasure in declaring this Oil Refinery officially open.

24

OPENING OF THE NATIONAL ASSEMBLY

October 15, 1963

When I last addressed this House on the 21st June, I invited you to ratify the Charter of African Unity, adopted by the Heads of African States at Addis Ababa in May this year. This Charter has now been formally notified by the Independent African States.

The tempo of development in Africa, since Addis Ababa, has been such that this Charter is already being overtaken by events. It has become clear that we must move forward quickly, with a united voice, to a Union Government of Africa.

In accordance with the spirit of the Charter, the African States have been able to present a unified front in the United Nations and at other international conferences. This unanimity, this community of vision, has not been easy. It has been achieved as a result of tedious consultations involving long delays and even the risk of failure to agree. Our actions would have been swifter, bolder and more effective if there had been in existence a strong, central political machinery for dealing with the wider problems affecting Africa as a whole.

Let us take the case of the Congo. For more than two years now I have advocated the policy that in the interest of the independence and sovereignty of the Congo, the situation in that country can best be solved by the African States themselves. It is significant in this connection that the African States were the first to land troops in the Congo in answer to the urgent appeal of the Congolese Government. Our troops have worked within the United Nations Organisation since the days of Lumumba. Now that the United Nations troops are about to be withdrawn from the Congo, the African States have an opportunity and an obligation to set an example of African self-help by going to the aid of a sister State. By so doing, we would have eliminated the rivalries of neo-colonialist and imperialist powers from the Congo.

I have accordingly proposed to the Government of the Congo, to the Secretary-General of the United Nations and to the Heads of the Independent African States and Government, that an all-African force should take over from the United Nations well in advance of its withdrawal from the Congo. Although this proposal was acceptable in principle, it could not be carried out because the African States, in spite of our resolutions at Addis Ababa, had not provided an effective machinery for such united action. The longer we delay action for a continental Government of Africa, the greater will be our troubles and our confusion.

Mr. Speaker, Members of the National Assembly: A continental political union for Africa is not only essential for our freedom and existence; it is necessary for the orderly progress and rapid development of our continent. African unity is the only solution to the vast problems facing our oppressed brothers and the Freedom Fighters in the Rhodesias, South Africa, Mozambique, Angola, South West Africa, Bechuanaland, Basutoland and Swaziland. It is the only solution to the difficulties which are bound to confront our newly independent States and those that are shortly to be independent.

As I speak to you now, there is a grim struggle—a battle for freedom—going on in Angola, Mozambique and Portuguese Guinea where the best of our youth are locked in mortal combat against the evil forces of colonialism in a determined effort to wipe out the pedigrees, the privileges the injustices, the principalities and the powers of a new imperialism.

It should be clear to the colonialists by now that we shall not give up the struggle until they leave Africa alone. If they do not leave Africa alone, we shall in our unity compel them to go. The struggle is not against race; it is against a system. The racialists and imperialists must quit Africa now.

As for the settlers, who continue to oppress our people under minority governments, it is time they came to terms with the African nationalists. We demand the acceptance of the democratic principle of one man, one vote. The will of the majority must forever prevail.

To achieve this end, we must hasten our goal of a united Africa. Only with our united strength can we free our oppressed compatriots from political bondage and from the shackles of imperialism and neo-colonialism.

When we of the emergent States of Africa and Asia talk of neo-colonialism we have no doubt about its meaning or its effect upon us. We live with it; to us it is no idle phantasy.

On the other hand, when the rich countries of the world talk of giving capital to the relatively poor countries, they wish to do this not only in a patronising way, but also in such a manner that they can use it to meddle in the affairs of the countries to which capital is offered. What they fail to realise is that capital in the form of so-called aid is not charity. It is given in hard commercial terms and should, therefore, not entitle those who give it to any political conditions whatsoever. In any case, it benefits both sides—the giver and the receiver, the investor and the country in which the capital is invested.

Those who wish to use this capital to bribe, influence, control and direct the affairs of African States are the neo-colonialists. They even try to dictate our budgets on their own terms. How can we maintain our economic development in this way?

Let us be very serious about this. As long as the world remains divided into rich and poor, exploiter and exploited, master and slave, developed and under-developed; as long as there are parts of the world whose resources can be exploited not for the welfare of the people of the area exploited, but for the benefit and in the interests of the rich and powerful foreign nations, the struggle for world peace stands undermined. Peace must be founded on a just appreciation of the need to extend the boundaries of human progress and human welfare so that the exploitation of nation by nation, of state by state, of race by race of man by man, shall forever cease.

Our struggles in Africa will have no meaning except in the context of world peace. That is why the Government of Ghana has welcomed and has become a party to the partial Test Ban Treaty recently adopted in Moscow by the nuclear powers. We are aware that this Treaty does not fulfil the hopes of mankind, and that it is only a small step towards the abolition of nuclear warfare. It must become a stepping stone to general and complete disarmament.

It is not enough to have a world without the bomb; we must press on to a world without war. We must rid ourselves as quickly as possible of the stocks and production facilities of nuclear, chemical, biological and other weapons of mass destruction. Only in a spirit of mutual confidence and trust among the nations, big and small, can we expect agreement on complete and total disarmament. It is in the confident expectation of such agreement being reached that we can redouble our efforts to build a happy and prosperous Ghana.

And now, Mr. Speaker and Members of the National Assembly: let us turn to our own domestic problems. Many of our people in several parts of Ghana have suffered and are still suffering considerable hardship from floods. I have therefore caused to be established a Civil Defence Committee. This Committee is dealing with the present situation and will also be available to deal with similar situations in the future.

Mr. Speaker, Members of the National Assembly: Our Seven-Year Development Plan will be launched shortly. Already we have established forty-five industrial projects, thirty-three of which are completely State owned; the rest are owned jointly by the State and private enterprises. Thirty-six more industrial projects are under examination or in construction.

We have a paper conversion factory in Takoradi, producing cardboard boxes, wrappers, paper bags, as well as toilet paper. We are importing paper and cardboard for its operations, but the next development will be to produce pulp out of local wood to feed the factory. Many of you may not know that we already have samples of paper produced from local wood. Very soon our pulping plants will be producing the pulp and paper to feed our printing machines. Our schools can then be supplied with exercise books made out of local paper and even text-books printed on locally produced paper.

Factories and industrial plants are springing up in Ghana with speed and ease. The wisdom and the efforts and sacrifices in the last ten years are now beginning to bear fruit. Can anyone of you call to mind what Ghana was like ten years ago? Can anyone of you now imagine what Ghana would have been like without the second port of Tema? Can anyone of you envisage the slowing down of our economic development if we had had to rely only on the port of Takoradi? Do you think we would have made the progress we are making if we had not embarked on our accelerated educational programme? Can anyone of you name the few places in the world where university education is as free as ours is? Can those of you who have long memories (those with short memories forget all too easily, anyhow!), looking back at the period just before independence, say in truth that we have not made progress? Progress there has been. Progress there continues to be; and progress there will be. Those who have eyes to see, let them see; and those who have ears to hear, let them hear.

I do not wish to parade before you our achievements within the last few years. I am only trying to point out the fact that our achievements since independence cannot easily be frowned upon even by our enemies and detractors.

The private sector of our industrial development continues to play a welcome role in our present economy. Ghana provides stable and steady opportunities for private investments provided investors are fair to us and accept the very fair conditions we have laid down for their operations.

We are determined that the industries we have already established and those we plan this year, should be operated efficiently by honest and reliable managers and workers, and that the goods produced shall be as good as any others. In order to achieve this, the structure, management, organisation and operations of all State industrial establishments will be reviewed and streamlined. Financial and production targets will be set for our productive enterprises, and everything will be done to ensure that those targets are reached, and even surpassed.

Mr. Speaker: Our investment policy has inspired confidence in our economic and political stability.

Work on the Volta River Project is running to schedule, and it is expected that the generation of electricity at the Dam site will commence by the end of 1965.

We are aware of the multi-purpose potentialities of the Volta River Project. A report prepared by a United Nations team on this aspect of the Project will be implemented. An Irrigation Department has been established within the Ministry of Agriculture, and a Power and Water Resources Department is being established within the Ministry of Works to investigate and make full use of our water resources.

Mr Speaker: Our decision to provide free basic text-books in primary, middle and secondary schools has been received with acclamation throughout the country. This is one example of the socialism we talk about in Ghana. We are resolved that every child shall have equal opportunity to develop his or her talents and capabilities to the utmost.

The education system left us by the colonial regime was designed to produce those persons best suited to serve the interests of a colonial power. In an independent Ghana, such an educational system is anachronistic. Education must be geared to our own aims, purposes and aspirations; to build a new society in which the best educational opportunities shall be the right of every citizen and the education of the individual shall be an opportunity for service. I recently appointed a Committee to review the whole basis of our pre-university educational system. The report of this Committee has been received and its recommendations are at present being examined for implementation.

Our universities have a vital part to play in our educational programme. Strength and power can only come to a people through education. Our universities must help to shape the destiny of the new Africa, and revitalise it from the springs of science and technology. The men and women who come from our institutions of higher learning should be imbued with a strong sense of service, devotion and loyalty to the Nation, in recognition of the great sacrifices that have been made for them by the Party and its Government.

In this connection, let it go on record that the Government of Ghana spends more on education in relation to our national income than any other country in the world.

During the coming year, the University of Ghana will establish several new Faculties, including a Nursing Tutors Faculty and Faculties in Political Science and Physical Education, to mention a few. A Medical Centre, which will include a Medical School, a Dental School, a teaching Hospital and facilities of the training of medical scientists and technicians, will shortly be established.

At the Kwame Nkrumah University of Science and Technology, several new courses, including Metallurgy and Sanitary Engineering, are being established. In order to fulfil Ghana's economic and industrial programmes, and to promote the well-being of our people, the Government has decided to award special additional scholarships in the following fields: Agronomy, Chemistry, Engineering, Geology and Physics.

The total student population in our three university institutions is now running over three thousand. In our primary, middle and secondary schools, the enrollment has quadrupled. Consider these changes. Look at what we have been able to do for ourselves as a nation. We are also making every effort to secure full employment for all. These are some of the things which we have tried to achieve through socialism. It is our only insurance against privation and want. We aim to create a society in which the maxim from each according to his ability and to each according to his work, shall apply, and in which the condition for the development of each shall be the condition for the development of all.

Mr. Speaker, in a developing country with vast potentialities and resources like Ghana, it is vital that our educational programme should be buttressed by an intensive study of science. Our need for scientists, engineers, doctors, architects and men with technological, skill, is enormous. Our industrial and agricultural revolution can only be effectively sustained if our training facilities for science and technical education are considerably expanded. We must ensure, therefore, that our children from their earliest stages in education, are given a lively interest in science and scientific pursuits. They must be taught to realise that science is not just something which works in the laboratory, but is all around us in nature and in the things we see in our daily lives.

For this reason, the Government will continue to give generous support to the Ghana Academy of Sciences and the Institutes attached to it, among which are the National Institute of Health and Medical Research, the Cocoa Research Station and the Building Research Institute. We believe the Academy of Sciences, by co-ordinating scientific research on a national scale, will enable us to make the maximum use of the facilities available to us for the advancement of science and technology.

The National Science Museum which is now under construction, will also assist greatly in this effort to inculcate in our young people a love for science and a spirit of discovery and adventure. When the Museum is opened early in 1965, it will be a source of inspiration to science teachers and students, as well as the general public.

Our general educational programme can be greatly enhanced by television, sound broadcasting and films.

Work on the National Television Service is progressing satisfactorily, and an experimental service will start by September, 1964. Our television programmes must reflect completely our culture, philosophy of life and national objectives. Television will be used to supplement our educational programmes, and to foster a lively interest in the world around us. Ghana's television will not cater for cheap entertainment nor commercialism; its paramount objective will be education in its broadest and purest sense.

Mr. Speaker, in the belief that the maintenance of a health society is of paramount importance for our national progress and welfare, the main emphasis in the Government's health policy will be on Preventive Medicine.

The structure of the Ministry of Health, and the working conditions of Government Medical Officers, will be revised in order to bring our medical services more into line with our needs at the present time. In particular the grade of "specialist" will be abolished, and all medical officers will have equal opportunity to acquire specialist experience and qualification in their own fields.

In future, all newly-qualified doctors, whether in Government service or intended for private practice, will be required to work initially for the State for at least two years. During this period, they will be posted to the rural areas to get first-hand experience in the treatment of tropical diseases. Doctors who are posted to rural areas in this way will be eligible for an allowance to be approved by the Government.

Maternity and Child Welfare Clinics will be established in selected parts of Accra and other main towns and cities. Ante-natal and major accident cases will be treated free of charge at all Government hospitals.

A National Accident Insurance Scheme will be established. Under this scheme all employees, whether employed by the State or in private service, will pay a prescribed fee every month in respect of free treatment in case of accident.

Hospital Management Boards will be established in respect of the major hospitals in the country. An immediate start will be made with Korle Bu.

A new Medical and Dental Council will be appointed. This Council will be given adequate powers, among other things, to set standards for medical education and practice, hospital administration, professional qualifications and registration. It will also serve as a disciplinary body and a watchdog for the ethics of the medical profession. Every effort would be made to enlist the sympathy and support of the many private doctors throughout the country in this new development.

After consultation with the Ghana Medical Association, it has been agreed that arrangements should be made, wherever possible, for private doctors and dentists to work for the Government for at least six hours in every week.

It has also been agreed that the fees charged by private doctors, dentist, pharmacists, midwives and nurses in private practice, shall be regulated and controlled. I have already established a Committee to deal with this matter.

Mr. Speaker: Malaria remains the biggest killer in Ghana. We must find the means to control it, if not to eradicate it completely from our midst. In this connection, a programme of aerial spraying will shortly be carried out in collaboration with the Ministry of

Health, the National Institute of Health and Medical Research and the Ghana Air Force in Greater Accra and other main centres.

We shall supplement this attack on the mosquito by an equally determined assault on the problem of water I have directed that a special programme should be prepared for providing our towns and villages with clean and adequate water supplies as soon as possible in an effort to free our people from water-borne diseases. If we can eradicate malaria and bring clean and wholesome water to our people everywhere, we shall be freed them from about eighty percent of the diseases which plague them.

Mr. Speaker, Members of the National Assembly: When recently I spoke at the Tenth Anniversary Celebrations of the United Ghana Farmers' Council Co-operatives, I stressed the importance of stepping up our food production in order to prevent our large imports of food. We must make every effort not to import the food we can grow here. Why import rice? Why import corn? And why import oranges?

We must, for this purpose, intensify work on our State Farms, on the Co-operative Farms, and encourage our peasant farmers to increase their production. The results of our efforts so far have been encouraging. All along the countryside, there are vast areas already under cultivation for rice, maize and vegetables Much, however, why we have established the Food Marketing Board in order to ensure that while the pressure to produce more food is maintained, the problems of distribution and food prices are well and carefully controlled and regulated.

Mr. Speaker: The cocoa industry continues to remain the backbone of our economy. Unfortunately for us, the world price for cocoa continues to be highly unsatisfactory. During the past main cocoa season we sold our cocoa at the very low average price of One Hundred and Sixty-three Pounds a ton. This is the lowest we have had to receive for a very long time. In spite of the increase in the volume and quality of our cocoa exports—including cocoa butter and cocoa paste—our earning from these exports remained unchanged. Our earnings from the export of cocoa beans alone was Sixty-seven Million Pounds. This is Two Million Pounds less than our receipts in 1961, although the crop exported was four per cent higher than in the previous year.

It is only when the price of cocoa reaches a world market price of about One Hundred and Eighty-six Pounds a ton that the Cocoa Marketing Board can afford to pay the fixed price of Seventy-two Shillings a load to the cocoa farmer without loss. It is clear, therefore, that when the Cocoa Marketing Board receives less than this amount for our cocoa, and as it did during the past main cocoa season, it is forced to run at a deficit. In spite of such losses, we have continued to honour our obligations to the farmers by paying them the guaranteed price.

Thus, the fall in the price of cocoa has put a considerable strain on our economy. Mainly as a result of import control restrictions, we have been able to improve our balance of payments position. In 1961 we had a deficit on current account of Fifty-two Million Pounds. Last year, as a result of the various measures we introduced, this deficit was reduced to Twenty-eight Million. The position is still improving, and our reserves now stand at nearly Seventy Million Pounds. Considering the staggering fall in the price of cocoa and the vast programmes of development we have undertaken, it is remarkable, and a credit to our Government, that we have been able to keep our reserves at this level.

Mr. Speaker, Members of the National Assembly: The tendency among us to buy imported goods in preference to the locally produced commodity is a relic of our colonial past. The colonialists bought our goods and returned them to us in the form of finished products which they sold to us on their terms. Just imagine the thought that our lime and oil are taken away only to be returned to us as lime juice and soap in gaily painted containers—and at what a price! In many cases the local product which we can now put on the market is as good as, if not better than, the imported product. It is certainly cheaper and fresher; in some cases it is even more potent.

Mr. Speaker: Our programme of industrialisation calls for huge capital outlays and for financial commitments which cannot show immediate results. Whenever we enter into a contract for an industrial project we have to make a down payment which may amount to ten percent, or more, of the agreed contract price. In addition to this initial payment, there are periodic payments which have to be made while the project is under construction. Sometimes we tend to get impatient, and to think that as soon as we announce that we have entered into an agreement to set up a factory, the products should be on the market almost immediately. Clearly there must be a period during which the plans are formulated and put into execution, during which the machines are installed and the wheels are made to turn for production. Within this period, there will inevitably be temporary shortages of some consumer goods, and here we, as a people—all of us—must be prepared to make sacrifices.

Mr. Speaker: We believe in progress and are determined to take our place among the developed nations of the world. We do not claim that we have not made mistakes in the past; we do not even claim that we shall not make mistakes in future. Nevertheless, we intend to proceed steadily and cautiously along the path which we have laid down for ourselves.

Mr. Speaker, Members of the National Assembly: For the 1963-64 Financial Year, Ministries and Departments have submitted estimates totalling One Hundred and Eighty-seven Million pounds. When you compare this figure to the approved estimates of nearly One Hundred and Twenty-eight Million Pounds for 1962-63, you will appreciate that the sums asked for represent an increase of approximately Fifty-eight Million Pounds over last year's estimates. I have therefore directed that these estimates should be reduced to more manageable proportions. I know that in doing so, I am restraining Departments and Ministries, all of which want to provide improved and expanded services. Much as I myself would like to see an expansion on all fronts, we must put a certain amount of restraint on expenditure of Ministries, Departments, State Enterprises and Institutions. This year we are all going to cut our coast according to our cloth.

Instead of One Hundred and Eighty-seven Million Pounds, the Minister of Finance will present to you a budget of approximately One Hundred and Forty-four Million Pounds. With proper economy, avoidance of waste and a greater sense of responsibility in the handling of State money and property, we shall be able to make this amount achieve the industrial, agricultural and economic goals we have set before us for the year.

Mr. Speaker: Government has decided that in future, all daily-rated workers who are employed on a permanent basis will be paid salaries on a monthly basis, instead of the present system of wages based on daily rates. Details of this new arrangement will be announced by the Minister of Finance.

Mr. Speaker, Members of the National Assembly: There is a tendency in most parts of the world to adopt a decimal system of reckoning. We in Ghana consider that it would be in our interest, too, to change from our present system of reckoning in pounds, shillings and pence, to a decimal system. This change will come into effect when the details have been worked out by the Ministry of Finance and the Bank of Ghana. We hope that it will be possible to make a beginning by July, 1965.

Mr. Speaker: Two years ago, as Members of the House will remember, Government introduced the Compulsory Savings Scheme by which everybody was required to contribute a portion of his emolument or income to a national savings scheme. Under this scheme all wage and salary earners contribute 5 percent of their current incomes, self-employed and professional people, as well as individual business and private companies, ten per cent on their income assessed for tax.

The Government has decided that the scheme should be abolished. The Minister of Finance will announce the details of this change when he makes his Budget Statement to the House.

Mr. Speaker: The requirement that companies should reinvest, sixty percent of their profits, after paying income tax, will no longer be enforced. We trust that companies, will, in spite of this decision continue to plough back into their businesses some of their profits, for expansion and improvement.

I have also directed that a financial amnesty should be granted in order that all those Ghanaians who still have investments abroad may repatriate such amounts to Ghana. I invite them to bring whatever savings they have abroad and invest them in Ghana, In this, way they will be assisting themselves and, at the same time, helping in the development of our country.

In spite of all you hear from those who have become professional grumblers and budget politicians, you can be sure that there is as yet no austerity or hardship in Ghana. I invite you to visit other countries to appreciate what austerity really means. If we have to forgo a few luxuries, it is because we have to opt for the terrific development now going on around us, as an investment for the future. We must also, bear in mind that in accordance with our socialist principles, those who are relatively well-to-do-must contribute more for the well-being of all. This principle will be emphasised in the budget. I trust that all, of you here will go back to your constituencies and impress upon the people the achievements of our Government and Party and the need to make an even greater effort to accelerate our development. I expect all our national newspapers will take up and expand on this theme for, the enlightenment of all their readers, that we are making great progress and that to continue with this progress we must bear our fair share of the burdens this advancement imposes on the men and f women who compose the Nation.

In this connection, Mr. Speaker, I have suggested that Members of Parliament should put their specialised skill and knowledge at the disposal of the Nation. Many of you in this House are teachers; some are pharmacists, university graduates, doctors, ministers of religion, surveyors, or hold qualifications in many other fields. You can participate actively in the building of our Nation by teaching, attending to the sick, working on the State Farms and in the factories and other State Enterprises. I have directed that Members of Parliament who accept such employment shall receive adequate remuneration for their services in addition to their parliamentary remuneration. As Members will appreciate, being a Member of Parliament is not a profession. During the period when the Assembly is not sitting, the country expects that you will combine your responsibilities to the constituencies with this kind of assistance to the Nation which I have suggested.

Let me remind you that no nation has become great or prosperous without sustained effort, hard work and sacrifices on the part of all its people. Let us not therefore have any doubts in our mind that the course we have charted is the right course, and that we must sail it with confidence in ourselves and our leaders.

Mr. Speaker: Our efforts to build a happy and prosperous Ghana; will be of no avail unless we uproot from our society the evils that retard our progress; for example, laziness and indifference. Our factories and other industrial projects, our farms and highways and educational institutions, are great symbols of material progress. Let us make them a success. Let us make sure that by our hard work they will be equal to the highest and the best in any part of the world. To be worthy of them, however, our own lives must reflect our best and noblest traditions and aspirations.

Let us see to it that these institutions do not become the bedrock of reaction and inertia. The principle socialism, namely collective responsibility for the welfare of all, must permeate every aspect of our nation's endeavour.

If we build for the future on the foundation of present made strong with the fabric of sound moral and spiritual life, we can be sure that our technological and scientific progress will lead us to real progress and happiness. Our strength and power should be measured not only in terms of our material growth and expansion, but also by the depth and intensity of the respect of our citizens for spiritual and moral values, their abhorrence of greed and the temptation for money, and their readiness to place themselves in the service of their fellow men.

We can only attain these ends through devotion to work and a sincere determination to do away with all forms of pride, arrogance and self-aggrandisement.

Ours is a society founded on a deep concern for the welfare of the masses here in Ghana and Africa. Let us continue to cherish the positive values of services, hard work, honest and integrity. As our community becomes more and more involved in the new complex of economic life, there is grave danger that the ties and loyalties in our traditional mode of living will be shaken, unless we make a conscious effort to revive and sustain them. The vices of modern civilization should be rigidly controlled.

Mr. Speaker, Members of the National Assembly: You, Members of this House, of this august Assembly, who are representatives of the people, have a solemn duty to lead this crusade for a better life in Ghana and happiness for its people. I now leave you to your deliberations. I pray that you will continue to be guided by Providence in the highest interests of our Nation.

UNITED NATIONS DAY

October 24, 1963

Today millions of people the world over celebrate the 18th anniversary of the United Nations Organisation. On this occasion, we in Ghana rededicate ourselves to the ideals and principles enshrined in the Charter of the United Nations Organisation. In some of its darkest hours we stood resolutely, in concert with nations of like mind behind the United Nations Organisation even when, at times, we could not agree with the way in which some of its objectives were implemented. We were able to do so because we believed, and still believe, that the United Nations Organisation, in spite of all its shortcomings, is the only universal instrument as yet devised by man for the reconciliation of differences among nations, and for the mobilization of world public opinion toward the achievement of these generally accepted objectives which are the foundations of the Charter. The success of the Organisation, of course, depends on the support of each of its members and their willingness to abide by, and to implement its decisions. This places a great responsibility on each member state of the Organisation—a responsibility for which they are individually accountable to mankind and to posterity.

Happily, the conclusion of the nuclear Test Ban Treaty offers great hope that mankind is on the threshold of a new era in which we may see the progressive elimination of tensions between nations and the establishment of World Peace. I am sure that all men of goodwill everywhere will share the joy of the gradual easing in world tension, and are ready to do their utmost for the achievement of complete disarmament, world prosperity and brotherhood.

Long Live the United Nations!

26
OPENING OF THE INSTITUTE OF AFRICAN STUDIES

Legon
October 25, 1963

I am very happy to be with you an this occasion and to welcome you to this official opening of the Institute of African Studies.

I regard this occasion as historically important. When we were planning this University, I knew that a many-sided Institute of African Studies which should fertilise the University, and through the University, the Nation, was a vital part of it.

This Institute has now been in existence for some time, and has already begun to make its contribution to the study of African history, culture and institutions, languages and arts. It has already begun to attract to itself scholars and students from Ghana, from other African countries and from the rest of the world.

The beginning of this present academic year marks, in a certain sense, a new development of this Institute. Already, the Institute has a team of seventeen research fellows and some forty post-graduate students—of whom about one-third come from Ghana and remainder from countries as diverse as Poland and the United States of America, Nigeria and Japan. We hope soon to have students and fellows from China and the Soviet Union.

This Institute is no longer an infant, but a growing child. It has begun to develop a definite character of its own; it is beginning to make itself known in the world. This, therefore, is a moment for taking stock and to think afresh about the functions of the Institute, and of the University within which it is set.

What sort of Institute of African Studies does Ghana want and have need of?

In what way can Ghana make its own specific contribution to the advancement of knowledge about the peoples and cultures of Africa through past history and through contemporary problems?

For what kind of service are we preparing students of this Institute and of our Universities?

Are we sure that we have established here the best possible relationship between teachers and students?

To what extent are our universities identified with the aspirations of Ghana and Africa?

You who are working in this Institute—as research workers and assistants, teachers and students—have a special responsibility for helping to answer these questions. I do, however, wish to take this opportunity to put to you some of the guiding principles which an Institute of African Studies situated here in Ghana at this period of our history must constantly bear in mind.

First and foremost, I would emphasise the need for a re-interpretation and a new assessment of the factors which make up our past. We have to recognise frankly that African studies, in the form in which they have been developed in the universities and centres of learning in the West, have been largely influenced by the concepts of old style "colonial studies," and still to some extent remain under the shadow of colonial ideologies and mentality.

Until recently the study of African history was regarded as a minor and marginal theme within the framework of imperial history.

The study of African social institutions and cultures was subordinated in varying degrees to the effort to maintain the apparatus of colonial power. In British Institutes of higher learning, for example, there was a tendency to look to social anthropologists to provide the kind of knowledge that would help to support the particular brand of colonial policy known as indirect rule.

The study of African languages was closely related to the practical objectives of the European missionary and the administrator.

African music, dancing and sculpture were labelled "primitive art." They were studied in such a way as to reinforce the picture of

African society as something grotesque, as a curious, mysterious human backwater, which helped to retard social progress in Africa and to prolong colonial domination over its peoples.

African economic problems, organisation, labour, immigration, agriculture, communications, industrial development were generally viewed from the standpoint of the European interest in the exploitation of African resources, just as African politics were studied in the context of the European interest in the management or manipulation of African affairs.

When I speak of a new interpretation and new assessment, I refer particularly to our Professors and Lecturers. The non-Ghanaian non-African Professors and Lecturers are, of course, welcome to work here with us. Intellectually there is no barrier between us and them. We appreciate, however, that their mental make-up has been largely influenced by their system of education and the facts of their society and environment. For this reason, they must endeavour to adjust and reorientate their attitudes and thought to our African conditions and aspirations. They must not try simply to reproduce here their own diverse patterns of education and culture. They must embrace and develop those aspirations and responsibilities which are clearly essential for maintaining a progressive and dynamic African society.

One essential function of this Institute must surely be to study the history, culture and institutions, languages and arts of Ghana and of Africa in new African-centred ways—in entire freedom from the propositions and pre-suppositions of the colonial epoch, and from the distortions of those Professors and Lecturers who continue to make European studies of Africa the basis of this new assessment. By the work of this Institute, we must re-assess and assert the glories and achievements of our African past and inspire our generation, and succeeding generations, with a vision of a better future.

But you should not stop here. Your work must also include a study of the origins and culture of peoples of African descent in the Americas and the Caribbean, and you should seek to maintain close relations with their scholars so that there may be cross fertilisation between Africa and those who have their roots in the African past.

The second guiding principles which I would emphasise is the urgent need to search for, edit, publish and make available sources of all kinds.

Ghanaian scholars who at an early period were actively concerned with the study of Ghana's history and institutions and helped to prepare the way for the creation of this Institute—such as Carl Reindorf, John Mensah Sarbah, Casely-Hayford, Attoh-Ahuma, Attobah Coguano, Anthony William Amu—understood how much the development of African Studies depended on the recovery of vital source material. Indeed, the search, publication and our interpretation of sources are obviously processes that must go hand in hand.

Among non-African students of Ghana's history and institutions, one of the most distinguished was undoubtedly Captain Rattray. By his intellectual honesty and diligence, he was able to appreciate and present to the world the values inherent in a culture which was, after all, foreign to him. It is impossible to respect an intellectual unless he shows this kind of honesty. After all, Academic Freedom must serve all legitimate ends, and not a particular end. And here the term "Academic Freedom" should not be used to cover up academic deficiencies and indiscipline.

I would therefore like to see this Institute, in co-operation with Institutes and Centres of African Studies in other African States, planning to produce what I would describe as an extensive and diversified Library of African Classics. Such a library would include editions, with translations and commentaries or works—whether in African, Asian or European languages—which are of special value for the student of African history, philosophy, literature and law. I can think of no more solid or enduring contribution which the Institute could make to the development of African Studies (on should lines) during the second half of the Twentieth Century, or to the training of future generations of Africanists.

Here in this Institute of African Studies you have already made a useful beginning with the collection of a substantial body of Arabic and Hausa documents. This collection has revealed a tradition of scholarship in Ghana about which little was previously known, and I hope that it will throw a new light on our history as part of the history of Africa.

I also regard as important the work which you are doing in the collection of stool histories and other forms of oral tradition—of poetry and African literature in all its forms—of which one admirable expression is Professor Nketsia's recently published book entitled "Folk Songs of Ghana," and Kofi Antubam's latest book on African culture. Other Ghanaians have done equally admirable work in this field. I may mention here Ephraim Amu whose work has created and established a Ghanaian style of music and revived an appreciation for it. Our old friend, J. B. Danquah, has also produced studies of Akan culture and institutions.

Much more should be done in this direction. There exists in our Universities, Faculties and Departments, such as Law, Economics, Politics, History, Geography, Philosophy and Sociology, the teaching which should be substantially based as soon as possible on African material.

Let us take an example. Our students in the Faculty of Law must be taught to appreciate the very intimate link that exists between law and social values. It is therefore important that the Law Faculty should be staffed by Africans.

There is no dearth of men and women among us qualified to teach in the Law Faculty. This applies equally to other Faculties. Only in this way can the Institute of African Studies fertilise the Universities and the Nation.

The magnitude of the changes taking place in Africa today is a positive index of the scale and pace necessary for our social reconstruction. Our Universities should provide us with the force and impetus needed to maintain this re-construction.

After years of bitter political struggle for our freedom and independence, our Continent is emerging systematically from colonialism and from the yoke of imperialism. The personality of the African which was stunted in this process can only be retrieved from these ruins if we make a conscious effort to restore Africa's ancient glory. It is only in conditions of total freedom and independence from foreign rule and interferences that the aspirations of our people will see real fulfilment and the African genius find his best expression.

When I speak of the African genius, I mean something different from Negritude, something not apologetic, but dynamic. Negritude consists in a mere literary affection and style which piles up word upon word and image upon image with occasional reference to Africa and things African. I do not mean a vague brotherhood based on a criterion of colour, or on the idea that Africans have no reasoning but only a sensitivity. By the African genius I mean something positive, or socialist conception of society, the efficiency and validity of our traditional statecraft, our highly developed code of morals, our hospitality and our purposeful energy.

This Institute must help to foster in our University educational, institutions the kind of education which will produce devoted men and women with imagination and ideas, who, by their life and actions, can inspire our people to look forward to a great future. Our aim must be to create a society that is not static but dynamic, a society in which equal opportunities are assured for all. Let us remember that as the aims and needs of our society change, so our educational institutions must be adjusted and adapted to reflect this change.

We must regard education as the "gateway to the enchanted cities of the mind," and not only as a means to personal economic security and social privilege. Indeed, education consists not only in the sum of what a man knows, or the skill with which he can put this to his own advantage. In my view, man's education must also be measured in terms of the soundness of his judgment of people and things, and in his power to understand and appreciate the needs of his fellow men, and to be of service to them. The educated man should be so sensitive to the conditions around him that he makes it his chief endeavour to improve these conditions for the good of all.

As you know, we have been doing a great deal to make education available to all. It is equally important that education should seek the welfare of the people and recognise our attempts to solve our economic, cultural, technological and scientific problems. In this connection, it will be desirable for your masters degree courses to be designed with such problems in mind. It is therefore important and necessary that our Universities and the Academy of Sciences should maintain the closest possible liaison in all fields. This will result not only in the efficient planning and execution of research, but also in economy in the use of funds and resources. Let me emphasise here that we look to the Universities to set an example by their efficiency and their sense of responsibility in the use of public funds. They must also set an example in loyalty to the Government and the people, in good citizenship, public morality and behaviour.

In order that the students may obtain the maximum benefit from their education in our Universities, it is imperative that the relationship between them and their teachers should be as free and easy as possible. Without this close interaction between mind and mind and the common fellowship of a University, it will be impossible to produce the type of student who understands the larger issues of the world around him.

Are we really sure that our students are in touch with the life of the nation? That they and their teachers fully appreciate what is going on in our society? The time has come for the gown to come to town.

In this connection, I can see no reason why courses should not continue to be organised at the Law School in Accra for Lay Magistrates, Local Government staff and other officers both in government and industry, who wish to acquire a knowledge of the law to assist them in their work. The staff of the Law Faculty in this university should be able to organise such courses for the benefit of the people in the categories I have mentioned.

It should also be possible for individual Lecturers and Professors on their own initiative to give lectures on subjects of their own choosing, to which the whole University and others outside it are invited. This would make possible the greatest freedom in discussion and the widest contacts between our Universities and the general public. I would like to see this become an established practice in our Universities.

Furthermore, I would stress the need for the Institute to be outward-looking. There may be some tension between the need to acquire new knowledge and the need to diffuse it—between the demands of research and the demands of teaching. But the two demands are essentially interdependent. And in Ghana the fact that we are committed to the construction of a socialist society makes it especially necessary that this Institute of African Studies should work closely with the people—and should be constantly improving upon its methods for serving the needs of the people—of Ghana, of Africa and of the world. Teachers and students in our Universities should clearly understand this.

What in practice does this mean? In part this objective—of serving the needs of the people—can be achieved by training this new generation of Africanists equipping them, through our Master of Arts and Diploma courses, with a sounder basis of knowledge in the various fields of African Studies than former generations have had. It is because of the great importance that I attach to the training of well-qualified Africanists who can feed back this new learning into our educational system that—in spite of the serious shortage of secondary school teachers—I have agreed that teachers who are selected for these post-graduate courses should be released for two years to take them.

An Institute of African Studies that is situated in Africa must pay particular attention to the arts of Africa, for the study of these can, enhance our understanding of African institutions and values, and, the cultural bonds that unite us. A comparative study of musical systems, for example, or the study of musical instruments, drum language, or the oral traditions that link music with social events, may illuminate historical problems or provide date for the study of our ethical and philosophical ideas.

In studying the arts, however, you must not be content with the accumulation of knowledge about the arts. Your researchers must stimulate creative activity; they must contribute to the development of the arts in Ghana and in other parts of Africa, they must stimulate the birth of a specifically African literature, which, exploring African themes and the depth of the African soul, will become an integral portion of a general world literature. It would be wrong to make this a mere appendage of world culture.

I hope that the School of Music and Drama, which works in close association with the Institute of African Studies, will provide this Institute with an outlet for creative work, and for the dissemination of knowledge of the arts through its extension and vacation, courses, as well as through regular full-time courses. I hope also that this

Institute, in association with the School of Music and Drama, will link the University of Ghana closely with the National Theatre movement in Ghana. In this way the Institute can serve the needs of the people by helping to develop new forms of dance and drama, of music and creative writing, that are at the same time closely related to our Ghanaian traditions and express the ideas and aspirations of our people at this critical stage in our history. This should lead to new strides in our cultural development.

There are other fields in which a great deal remains to be done. In addition to publishing the results of its research in a form in which it will be available in scholars, the Institute must bo concerned with its diffusion in a more popular form among a much wider public. While there are many channels through which this new learning can be spread—including radio and, in the very near future, television—I am particularly anxious that the Institute should assist the Government in the planning and production of new textbooks for use in our secondary schools, training colleges, workers' colleges and educational institutions generally.

I have attempted to indicate briefly some of the principles which should guide the institute in its work. It is for you to develop, amplify and apply these in relation to the actual possibilities that present themselves to you. Of one thing I am sure, that Ghana offers a rich and exciting field of work and a friendly and sympathetic environment for scholars and students from any part of the world who wish seriously to devote themselves to a study of African and African civilisations.

Hence it will, I hope be possible to say of this Institute—and indeed, of our Universities—as the historian Mahmut Kati said of another famous centre of learning—16th Century Timbuktu—I quote: "In those days Timbuktu did not have its equal—from the province of Mali to the extreme limits therein of Maghrib, for the solidity of its institutions, its political liberties, the purity of its morals, the security of persons, its consideration and compassion towards the poor and towards foreigners, its courtesy towards states and men of learning and the financial assistance which it provided for the latter. The scholars of this period were the most respected among the Believers for their generosity, their force of character, and their discretion."

Finally, I would hope that this Institute would always conceive its function as being to study Africa, in the widest possible sense—Africa in all it complexity and diversity, and its underlying unity.

Let us consider some of the implications of the concept of African unity for the study of African peoples and cultures, and for the work of your Institute.

It should mean, in the first place, that in your research and your teaching you are not limited by conventional territorial or regional boundaries. This is essentially an Institute of African Studies, not of Ghana Studies, nor of West African Studies. Of course you are bound to take a special interest in exploring the history, institutions, languages and arts of the people of Ghana, and in establishing these studies on a sound basis—as indeed you are already doing.

But these investigations must inevitably lead outwards—to the exploration of the connections between the musical forms, the dances, the literature, the plastic arts, the philosophical and religious beliefs, the systems of government, the patters of trade and economic organisation that have been developed here in Ghana, and the cultures of other African peoples and other regions of Africa. Ghana, that is to say, can only be understood in the total African context.

Let me illustrate this point.

As you know, Ghana has always been one of the great gold-producing areas of the world. Much of the gold from our mines was exported by our people, who conducted this trade as an exclusive state enterprise, to Jenne on the Niger, whence it was transported by canoe down the Niger to Timbuktu—the great entrepot and meeting-place of river-borne and desert-borne traffic. At Timbuktu the gold was transferred to the camel caravans, which carried it across the Sahara to the commercial centres of Western Maghrib—whence part would be re-exported to Western Europe.

It was normal for African trading firms to have their agents in Jenne and Timbuktu, in Marrakesh and Fez with trade northwards as far as England. This, in the early nineteenth century we find in Timbuktu, the home of the University of Sankore, merchants visiting their business colleagues in Liverpool, while merchants from North Africa took part in trade missions to Kumasi.

Another distinct commercial network had grown up around the cola trade, linking Ghana and its neighbours with the Hausa State and Bornu, and thus—by the central Sahara trade routes—with Tripoli and Tunis.

These commercial contacts were naturally reflected at the level of culture. The languages, literature, music, architecture and domestic arts of Ghana have made their import in a great variety of ways, through these ancient links on the wider African world, and beyond.

Very few of you may know, for example, that Baden Powell based the idea of the Boy Scout Movement, including the left-hand shake, on the concept of Ashanti military strategy and youth organisation.

Consider a Ghanaian writer like Al-Hajj 'Umoru, who lived from about 1850 to 1934, some forty of whose Arabic works, in poetry and prose, have so far been collected by the Institute of African Studies. Al-Hajj 'Umoru, belonged to a family of Hausa traders and scholars—his great-grandfather had taken part in 'Uthman dan Fodio's revolution. Born and educated in Kano, he travelled along the kola route to Salaga where he settled as a young man and built up a school of Arabic and Koranic studies; at the time of the Salaga wars, he migrated to Kete-Krachi; well-read in classical Arabic Literature, he collected around him students from various parts of West Africa, and described in some of his poems the disintegration of African society consequent upon the coming of British.

Similarly, we cannot hope to understand adequately the medieval civilisations of West Africa-ancient Ghana, Mali, Songhay, Kanem, Bornu, Oyo—without taking full account of the civilisations which emerged in Eastern, Central and Southern Africa—Meroe, Aksum, Adal, Kilwa, Monomotapa, Mogadishu, Malindi, Mombasa, Zanzibar, Pemba, Chang, Amir exploring the problems of their interconnections, their points of resemblance and difference. In North Africa, too, powerful enlightened civilisations had grown up in Egypt, Libya, Tunisia, Algeria and Morocco.

These cities, states and empires developed their own political institutions and organisations, based on their own conceptions of the nature and ideals of society. These institutions and organisations were so efficient, and their underlying ideas so valid, that it is surely our duty to give them their place in our studies here.

Nor must the concept of African unity be thought of in a restrictive sense. Just as, in the study of West African civilisations, we have to examine their relationships, by way of the Sahara, with North Africa and the Mediterranean world, so, in studying the civilisations of Eastern and Southern Africa, we have to recognise the importance of their relationships, by way of the Indian Ocean, with Arabia, India, Indonesia and China.

The 11th Century Arab geographer, Al-Bakri, who gave the first full account of the ancient Empire of Ghana, also gave the first description of the Czech city of Prague.

When we turn to the study of modern Africa we are again confronted with the necessity of thinking in continental terms. The liberation movements which have emerged in Africa have clearly all been aspects of a single African revolution. They have to be understood from the standpoint of their common characteristics and objectives, as well as from the standpoint of the special kinds of colonial situation within which they have had to operate and the special problems which they have had to face.

So, while of course no single institution can possibly attempt to cover the whole range of African Studies in all their multiplicity and complexity, I hope to see growing up here in this Institute a body of scholars with interest as many-sided and diversified as our resources can allow. We should in time be able to provide for our students here opportunities for the study of the history, the major languages and literatures, the music and arts, the economic, social and political institutions, of the entire African continent—so that, though individual students will necessarily have to specialise in particular fields, there will be no major sector of African Studies that will be unrepresented here.

This is not, I think, too ambitious an aim. And I am glad to know that the Institute is already taking steps to develop research and teaching both in North African and in East African History—with their prerequisites, Arabic and Swahili.

At the same time, we must try to ensure that there is the same kind of diversity among the student body. While we are glad to welcome students from Asia, Europe and the Americas, we have naturally a special interest in developing this Institute as a centre where students from all parts of Africa can meet together and acquire this new learning-and thus take their places among the new generation of Africanists which Africa so urgently needs; where the artificial divisions between so-called "English-speaking," "French-speaking," "Portuguese-speaking" Africans will have no meaning.

The *Encyclopaedia Africana,* sponsored by the Ghana Academy of Sciences, should provide a forum for African scholars working together and seeking forth the results of their research and scholarship.

Scholars, students and friends: the work on which you are engaged here can be of great value for the future of Ghana, of Africa and of the world. Here let me pay tribute to your Director, Thomas Hodgkin, for the energy and thought with which he has carried out his work. It is to his credit that such a firm foundation has been laid at this Institute.

Ladies and Gentlemen: I now have great pleasure in declaring the Institute of African Studies formally and officially open.

27

OPENING OF THE SECOND CONFERENCE OF AFRICAN JOURNALISTS

November 11, 1963

On behalf of the Government and people of Ghana, and on my own behalf, let me welcome you, journalists of Africa, and all those who have come here to attend this conference.

It is not simply out of courtesy that I am here to open this Conference of African Journalists. Most of you will know that I come to speak to you with a particular sense of pleasure as an old journalist who can still be excited by the smell of the printer's ink and the clatter of the printing machine.

If we interpret journalism as the dissemination of news and the clarion to action, then journalism is certainly not new to Africa.

From time immemorial we have developed our own special system of transmitting news and messages across the country, from village to village, from community to community; we have devised our peculiar means of gathering our people together and putting problems before them for decision. The talking drums and the courier have been the harbingers of news. From the days of the drum, we have accepted as an inexorable canon that the news which was transmitted should be true and the information conveyed accurate and reliable. For the safety and the lives of many people might depend upon it.

In these modern days, we have the teleprinter and the telex machine for conveying news at greater speed. But the principle and the purpose of it all remain the same. Even while the drum spoke, we in Africa were developing more modern forms of journalism.

Indigenous newspapers in West Africa have at least a hundred years of history behind them. In 1858, only fourteen years after the Bond of 1844 and before the Gold Coast had been annexed as a definitive colony of Great Britain the *West African Herald* was edited by Charles Bannerman, a son of the soil. About the same time, John Tengo Jabavu was editing the *IMVO* in South Africa. In Nigeria, the basic ideas of modem nationalism were developed by John Payne Jackson from 1891, in his journal, *The Lagos Weekly Record*.

James Brew in the Gold Coast of the 1870's and 80's, and J. E. Casely Hayford, a generation after, edited local, nationalist papers; but they were restricted in their circulation to the few literate readers along the coast.

The astonishing thing about these editors and their small band of journalistic collaborators was how they managed to build up a secret intelligence and news gathering service along the coast, which involved, beside the normal hazards of anti-colonialist activity, the danger of some of them finding a premature watery grave. In those days, there was no proper road between Cape Coast and Accra—not even the rough one we knew before the Government of the Convention People's Party built the present modern ones. So the editors and their co-workers worked their clandestine way by canoe along the coast to the capital, Accra. There they ferretted out all the latest material that could be used against the colonialist government, and then they paddled their dangerous way back to Cape Coast. All these activities were done at night. It was always a puzzle to the British administration in Accra as to how these newspapers were able to appear in Cape Coast with such "hot" news so quickly.

Nevertheless, these and other journalists did much to spread the doctrine of equal rights for Africans, especially as schooling began to widen out gradually and we were becoming conscious of ourselves as political beings.

In North Africa, in 1930, *L'Action Tunisienne* was launched by Habib Bourgiba, now President of Tunisia, and a group of his Neo Destour party members. In the Ivory Coast in 1935, the journal *L'Eclaireur* had an immense success in African circles. It led a campaign against reactionary chiefs and colonialist oppression. It demanded measures of social reconstruction and urged the cause of the unemployed and of the African farmers, who had been hit by the colonialist-made economic crisis. Nnamdi Azikiwe's *West African Pilot* and the organ of the Convention People's Party—the Accra

Evening News—in more recent years, led in the field of nationalist journalism. Wallace Johnson of Sierra Leone, with his *West African Standard,* did some ground work in trade union journalism. *The Africanist* emerged as the custodian of South African nationalism in 1953 and remained a revolutionary mouthpiece of the Africans of South Africa. Its founder and first editor was Managaliso Sobukwe, President of the Pan-Africanist Congress of South Africa, who is now detained indefinitely on Robben Island after serving three years' imprisonment for his part in the cause of freedom.

George Padmore, working outside Africa, but identifying himself completely with its struggles, carried on almost all of his adult life a tenacious fight for African nationalism and independence. His contributions to the press of Africa and to that of peoples of African descent in the West Indies and the United States; his widespread journalistic writings throughout the world, served as rallying point and inspiration to the leaders of African independence and the masses.

The African press, born of incipient nationalism, nurtured on political consciousness, and developed side by side with a growing sense of responsibility, is now strong and healthy, despite the many obstacles placed in its way. However, the fact that the press in Africa to-day is an important and influential institution, does not alone lend importance to your meeting to-day.

The special significance of this gathering is that it is the first conference of African Journalists since the Organisation of African Unity was established at Addis Ababa in May this year

As such it can do nothing less than fulfil the purpose of a continental press conference on the Unity of Africa.

As a professional man, the African journalist shares with other journalists throughout the world, the duty of gathering information carefully and of disseminating it honestly. To tamper with the truth is treason to the human mind. By poisoning the well-springs of public opinion with falsehood, you defeat, in the long run, your own ends. Once a journal gains a reputation for even occasional unreliability or distortion, its value is destroyed.

It is part of our revolutionary credo that within the competitive system of capitalism, the press cannot function in accordance with a strict regard for the sacredness of facts, and that the press, therefore, should not remain in private hands.

As, in a capitalist or—neo-colonialist environment, profit from circulation and advertising is the major consideration, the journalist working within it is caught by its mechanics.

No matter how great his personal integrity, as long as he remains, he must mould his thinking to its dictates. Consciously or unconsciously, he is forced into arranging news and information to fit the outlook of his journal. He finds himself rejecting or distorting facts that do not coincide with the outlook and interest of his employer or the medium's advertisers. Willy-nilly, he adjusts his ideas to that of the class which his journal represents, the class for which it caters, the interests and objectives which it serves to advance.

Under the pressure of competition for advertising revenue, trivialities are blown up, the vulgar emphasised, ethics forgotten, the important trimmed to the class outlook. Enmities are fanned and peace is perverted. The search is for sensation and the justification of an unjust system in which truth or the journalist must become the casualty.

It is no wonder, then, that for every decent or well-informed journal in a capitalist country, you have many more of the kind that concentrates on sensationalism and scandal; that cover up facts or deny them; that manufacture news in order to mislead and corrupt. There are journals that employ special techniques of presentation in order to ensnare the minds not just of thousands, but of the millions that read them. Every means, both subtle and raw, are used to maintain sway over the minds of men, and thus secure and hold their support in the continued exploitation and suppression of the oppressed. Oft times they are led to concur in their own exploitation. They are enjoined against peace, they are manoeuvred against freedom and right.

Unfortunately, some of these journals have made their way into our continent and are employing their influence to wean our people to ideas and ways of life that run counter to our image and our hopes. We must be vigilant against their penetration and their incitement. We must be careful not to take their falsities as models, either for our public or our journalists. For our African journalists have; different task, a higher responsibility, a greater objective, which demand a mould of quite another order.

In Africa today, three types of African journalists can be recognised on our continent. There are those who are purposefully and unreservedly devoted to the cause of the African Revolution. Such journalists are dedicated to African freedom, African progress an African unity.

Then, there are those who by their work serve only the interests of private capital. These journalists have no minds of their own, no devotion to their people or their continent. They carry out the dictates of their foreign employers operating in Africa; they gyrate in the effort to anticipate their masters' wishes.

Thirdly, there are those journalists who, unwittingly, or deliberately, serve the interests of foreign governments by their support of the client and puppet regimes that have been established in Africa.

The last two categories wrap their distortions and their diversions from the truth in a morbid appeal to chauvinism, unreason and latent animosities.

Whether they are aware of it or not, they are misusing their talents and their opportunity in the interest of Africa's enemies and against those of our people, our continent and our cause.

We who are fighting against colonialism and imperialism, we who are fighting against the blandishment of client states and settler governments in Africa, and are seeking to create a just society in which the welfare of each shall be the welfare of all, must stand against the methods of those whose journalism has precisely the opposite ends. We have nothing to gain by suppressing or distorting facts. Circulation of itself is not our first consideration; though obviously we are anxious to reach and inform the widest possible audience. But we have no wish to play upon the gullibility of that audience, for it is precisely to the interests of that audience that we are dedicated. And we can only promote those interests by self-criticism and the faithful presentation of truth and fact.

The journalist who works faithfully for our African Revolution refuses to sell his soul to imperialism and to Moloch, and thus starts with an advantage over his colleagues of the imperialist and neo-colonialist press.

His integrity, as long as he persists in this decision, is assured. To the true African journalists, his newspaper is a collective organiser, a collective instrument of mobilisation and a collective educator—a weapon, first and foremost, to over-throw colonialism and imperialism, and to assist total African independence and unity.

The true African journalist, abjuring imperialist blandishments and bribes, can certainly call his soul his own. His work may be more difficult because of deficiencies in the technical means of gathering information and the daily harassments that confront him; his remuneration may not be great and expense accounts non-existent. But he has other, more satisfying rewards. He draws contentment from an honest job honestly done. His satisfaction is in his integrity, in work performed for the betterment of his fellows and the society of which he is a worthy member.

He does not need to peep through keyholes for scandals, or bribe underlings to divulge what should remain private and personal; he does not need to concoct or manufacture exciting revelations. He is not forced to doctor news and debase pubic standards to fit the purpose of the rich and the world-be richer. I am reminded here that a British journalist friend of mine once told me that sometimes the news items he sent to his paper in London were so doctored that he had difficulty in recognising what he himself had written. The true African journalist very often works for the organ of the political party to which he himself belongs and in whose purpose he believes. He works to serve a society moving in the direction of his own aspirations.

How many journalists of the imperialist and neo-colonialist press have this satisfaction? How many know this peace of mind? How many work with a respect for their calling, and with faith in the society which they serve?

These are high rewards for an honest man in the course of his professional career. But they are not earned without corresponding responsibilities. Every African is responsible to the African Revolution by the heritage of his birth and by his experience of colonialism and imperialism.

The responsibilities of the journalist come particularly high in the hierarchy of our revolution; none higher, none more onerous, none more satisfying than those of an African journalist using his talents and his integrity in adverse and sacrificing conditions, not only in the cause of the freedom and independence of his country, but in the wider cause of the political unity and cultural and material development of the African continent, of which his country is a part.

Truth, we say, must be the watchword of our African journalists and facts must be his guide. These tenets, however, must not excuse dullness in our newspapers and our journals. They must not be used as a cover for shoddy writing and ambiguous intentions. The African journalist is not only expected to communicate the facts and aims of our African Revolution, but to do so compellingly and without fear. He must continually and fearlessly expose neo-colonialist subterfuge. He must attain a proper understanding of the African Revolution, its purpose and its travails. He must acquire technical proficiency and literary skill.

Even though he tells the truth, it does not make the same impact when presented in a dull manner with vain repetition, as if without conviction.

We must make our publications attractive to the eye and easy to handle and read. We cannot self-righteously or contemptuously dismiss the appeal or under-rate the seductiveness of the brightness in which the imperialism clothes its journalistic offerings. Bright colours and gay forms are used to cover insidious suggestiveness. We have more genuine fare to offer, but we would be foolish to dismiss airily the blandishments that cover their frivolities and poisonous intentions. We would be deceiving ourselves if we were to under-rate their abilities and their determination to penetrate deeply into our midst and draw our people away from their own true interests.

Africa presents a vast market for popular magazines—especially the smart magazines which cater for the faster juvenile and middle-class Afro-Americans, anxious to share in the fruits of the rich material environment so near and yet so far from their reach. Our enemies are intent to make these the thin edge of intellectual neo-colonialism.

You will not beat the spurious and seductive output of Western journalism except by publications of high quality and popular appeal. The answer is not to copy them but to excel them—to educate the taste of the African reader to the point of rejecting the undesirable foreign wares.

To do this, however, you must understand our Revolution, know its mainsprings and its objectives. You must know what spirit we have to import, what kind of society we are seeking, what nature of, men and women we hope to fashion. The facts you gather must manifest Revolution, foster its clan and depict truthfully its progress, its pitfalls and obstacles. They must encourage our people and not deceive them with false hopes or false achievements.

You have the duty to express the views which will move our Revolution forward. For all of this, the ordinary professional education of a journalist is not enough. You must understand the relationship between the press and our society and you must understand our society in relation to the rest of the world.

The truly African revolutionary press does not exist merely for the purpose of enriching its proprietors or entertaining its readers. It is an integral part of our society, with which its purpose is in consonance. Just as in the capitalist countries the press represents and carries out the purpose of capitalism, so in Revolutionary Africa, our Revolutionary African press must present and carry forward our revolutionary purpose. This is to establish a progressive political and economic system upon our continent that will free men from want and every form of social injustice and enable them to work out their social and cultural destinies in peace and at ease. This is what we are trying to do here in the Ghana School of Journalism.

For our continent to develop along these lines, we must repel a host of enemies. Enemies whom we call imperialists, colonialists and neo-colonialists, in an attempt to categorise their activities, but enemies whose ends are always the same: the undermining and restriction of our independence. They work laboriously to impede and frustrate our economic development; they employ all manner of means to prevent our unity as a continent. To destroy our political stability is the obvious method of attacking our independence.

Hence they try to corrupt our political institutions, our civil service, our police, our army. Even our universities and judiciary are not exempt from their attempts to capture our constitution for their own ends through bribery and corruption. But thanks to the firm resistance at all levels of our national movements, they are often foiled.

A more effective method of destroying our political stability is to intensify our poverty so that popular dissatisfaction will infect our states with treason and violence. The legacies of poverty and backwardness, left by the colonialists and which can be removed only by great sacrifices spread over long periods, offer fertile fields for such intrigue.

We have seen enough to know that the imperialists use decolonisation as a manoeuvre for the greater exploitation of their former colonies. They do not accept it as a historical necessity to end a shameful and untenable period in human history. In the face of stormy winds of freedom blowing through Africa, the colonialists have only veered their course; they have not changed it. Where once they ruled by force, they now manipulate to maintain their hold (on Africa) by cunning, bribery and subterranean violence.

Ironically, they follow in the footsteps of the early Portuguese explorers, who first named the southern tip of our continent the Cape of Storms, and then changed the name to the Cape of Good Hope. The change of name could not change the weather conditions; and did no more for the indigenous inhabitants than to make that corner of Africa a hell on earth for them.

If the imperialists have been forced by circumstances to cede independence to former colonies, we know by now that the intention was to make that independence purely nominal. Wherever independence aims to become a reality, the hostility of the imperialists knows no bounds. This ulterior intention has resulted in dividing Africa into client states and states whose independence hangs by a thread.

As colonialism vanishes away from Africa under the blows of Freedom Fighters, neo-colonialism is raising its head as the greatest threat to our freedom and progress.

What is neo-colonialism? It is the situation we find in a country where a colonial power grants nominal political independence to a territory, but sees to it that the control of the economic arrangements of the territory are still in the hands of the ex-colonial power; which is thereby able to dominate its economy and, indirectly, the state apparatus. It is empire-building without the flag.

And this is how it works:

They see to it that the political power remains in the hands of indigenous reactionaries.

They manoeuvre to control the Army, the Police and even the Intelligence Services.

They see to it that the economic institutions of the country are in the hands of their agents, and that economic production is completely controlled by private foreign capital leaving only the less profitable infrastructure in the hands of the indigenous population.

They divide the Trade Union and other popular movements.

When they have gained full control, in this way, of a client or puppet state, with a client or puppet administration, then they are in a position to do what they like to the territory, its government and its people.

If they cannot get their own way, then they engineer political and military coups, to overthrow the regimes and install new reactionary regimes which will carry out their orders.

Some of us allow ourselves to be used as agents of such neo-colonialist and settler government espionage systems operating in Africa. Even the Fascist Regime of South Africa could have agents among us here.

I have always been particularly proud of my trade union associations. As a worker in my student days in America, I belonged to the Maritime Workers' Union and played an active part in our struggles to better the living conditions of our fellow workers.

From the very early days of the African resistance struggle, trade unions have played a dominant role in the conquering liberation movements. That is our experience in Ghana, and I know the experience throughout the other African countries.

Throughout this vast continent of ours, workers organised or unorganised must become aware of the duty they owe not only to their own country but to mother Africa and must rapidly adjust themselves to the new role of nation building and also guard jealously our independence against incursions of neo-colonialism. African workers must organise themselves for the final overthrow of colonialism and liquidation of neo-colonialist or neo-colonialist exploitation. The journalists of Africa must recognise this and use the African press in supporting our trade unions and exposing the evils of neo-colonialism.

My faith in the All-African Trade Union Federation as the most positive and reliable ally in our struggle against neo-colonialism is an abiding one. AATUF must have the unconditional support of the African Press as against the other neo-colonialist trade union groupings in Africa, either of ICFTU or those who serve as vehicle of neo-colonialist infiltration. Our African journalists must help explain the importance of trade unions in our African revolution. The African trade unions are those that have their roots in the broad mass of our people. They must be in a position to bring to our attention quickly the feelings of the workers and we must draw them into consultation on the formulation of Government policy. There cannot be any conflict of interest in the task of nation building. It must be the responsibility of the African Governments to encourage our trade unions and help them consolidate their strength.

To build Africa which must be Africa liberated from exploitation, Africa just and strong, we must build with the people and for the people.

Africa must win through to real independence; and the only road open to us is the one whose first station was the Summit Conference of Addis Ababa. We must now press on quickly to a Union Government of Africa.

Those who say that a continental government of Africa is illusory are deceiving themselves. Worse, they are deceiving their people, who see in the unity of our continent the way to a better life. They ignore the lessons of history. If the United States of America could do it, if the Soviet Union could do it, if India could do it, why not Africa?

And it needs to be done now. No useful purpose is served by putting it off. On the contrary, recent events have shown that delay can only exacerbate our divisions and make our coming together more difficult.

We want the widest economic and social development, and we want it as soon as possible. We can get it, and get it quicker, only by planning it on a continental scale. And it becomes more and more obvious that continental planning cannot precede but must emanate from a continental government of Africa. It is this recognition that directs our enemies and detractors to keep us divided.

An All-African High Command is an immediate necessity, so that we can be ready at all times to protect our sovereignty and our independence. Otherwise, we will fight among ourselves, and destroy all we have so far achieved, to the delight and advantage of the neo-colonialists.

Only a continental government of Africa will give reality and purpose to African Unity. Without it, African Unity will remain an empty and sentimental slogan.

How can we hope to stop France from continually testing atom bombs in the Sahara? Only a Continental Government of Africa can make de Gaulle's France pause to reflect. No resolutions or charters can hope to do this.

A continental government for Africa, backed by a continental army under a unified High Command, would have authority to keep the peace throughout Africa. It would close the road now wide open to a neo-colonialist take-over in Africa.

The Moroccan-Algerian border dispute which erupted into open warfare last month, and others like it, present a grave symptom of our desperate plight as independent states. Among the colonial legacies which imperil our present and our future, there is the uneasy condition of ill-defined boundaries between states which hug a nationalist passion and new-found independence. What can more easily lead to strife, conflict and war?

With all the goodwill and wise leadership in the world, these border disputes cannot be permanently settled. Especially when they have their origin in the criminal colonial scramble for Africa. Why visit the sins of colonialism upon the children of the African Revolution? Why should we pay for the sins that colonialists have committed against us? The only solution to such border disputes lies in the establishment of a Union Government of Africa in which we shall all enjoy a common union citizenship which will make boundaries melt away.

We were divided on our continent not by chance or by choice, but by force. We cannot cure that division by force among ourselves. We can only cure it by African unity, by coming together within a union government, not by perpetuating the artificial boundaries between us.

In the face of the assaults which neo-colonialism is now making on the whole of Africa, and the preparations for war in those parts of Africa still occupied by the imperialists, the dividing line between triumph and disaster for African unity surmounted by a continental government is very thin. The military coups and plots, the border disputes in independent Africa do not help to correct this situation.

We have allowed the neo-colonialists to intimidate us and make us afraid to move on to a continental government in Africa. While we listen to their counsels about the difficulties and the inopportuneness; while we allow them to convince us that there are too many differences between us; while we permit them to assure us that we can only prosper by being strung to them and not to ourselves; they are getting on with their plans to drive us further and further apart and deepen the fits between us.

Time is being used by them to sow confusion and destruction among us. We can frustrate their knuvish tricks only by coming together, by coming together now. Putting off the reality of African Union will only add inertia to the confusion, it will bring the African revolution to a standstill, perhaps for the next thousand years. Now is the hour to seal the Union Government of Africa.

This is the Africa which you, as African journalists, must help to create and develop, the new Africa of which our people dream, for which they stretch out their hands. With your brains and your pens, with the strength of your faith and the passion of your thoughts and words, you are the vanguard of the crusade for a United Africa. Never sell yourselves for a mess of pottage; never allow yourselves to be bought.

Less than six months have elapsed since Addis Ababa and, as I said the other day, the course of events has already overtaken us. We must take care that it does not overwhelm us completely. If there has been an ebb in the full tide of continental unity which launched the Addis Ababa Charter, we must attribute it to pressure on the client states and to a general stepping up of imperialist intrigues and threats throughout Africa.

Let us, for example, take the Congo—that large and rich state in the heart of Africa—as the yardstick by which to measure whether we have progressed or not since the Summit Conference. If we look closely, we will see no progress, but rather a slackening of the high resolves and practical measures which we enunciated at Addis Ababa.

The situation in the Congo approximates that which found the Latin American states engulfed in political and military coups by juntas in the pay of outside interests and the control of foreign intelligence agencies.

The Belgian exploiters return in droves, secure in the knowledge that Mobutu's army is the only source of governmental power, and that he will protect them if the people's fury erupts. American and Belgian capitalist have now resolved their differences in the Congo, whose wealth they mean to exploit as joint partners once a military dictatorship has broken completely the Lumumbaist political forces and the resistance of the industrial workers.

The writing on the wall for the Congo is as plain as it was in Peru, as it was in the Dominican Republic and in Honduras—as it was in South Vietnam before the military junta took over in order to give the war against the people of Vietnam a new lease of life.

The plight of the Congo is no secret in Africa. It is known in the fullest detail in every part of the world. What will happen if we allow the Congo Republic to go the way of a Latin American Republic? We shall do no less than give the green light for the consortium of imperialists now operating in Africa to go ahead with plans for the structure of neo-colonialism here on the Latin American model.

If we let go the Congo it will strengthen the colonialists and the settler-government of Southern Africa. It will mean the handing over of the struggle of our brothers in Northern and Southern Rhodesia and in South Africa and the Protectorates to the more ruthless persecution of the practitioners of apartheid and quasi-apartheid. It will give encouragement to Verwoerd and his allies to strengthen still further the army that is being built up in South Africa.

This is the time we should be getting together to coalesce our forces against the threat of apartheid South Africa's menace to our African independence. We would be foolish if we sit back calmly while South Africa's ground to air missile base endangers our very existence.

If we let go the Congo we shall reinforce neo-colonialist presence here in Africa. While we are dilly-dallying, they are getting busier and busier on our continent. Western Powers are increasing their investments in South Africa and refuse to be deflected from their support of Verwoerd and his regime. Surely these are signs of imperialist strength and unity, while we demonstrate our divisions and our feebleness.

If we let go the Congo we shall nullify the Addis Ababa Charter and confuse our minds with the hope of a unity that will never be fulfiled. We shall hand to neo-colonialist an instrument that will help them rather than the unity of Africa. The Congo is a symbol to all of us. And what goes on there now may be a symbol of what can happen to Ghana, or Nigeria, or Guinea, or Mali, or Tanganyika or any other African state.

It is against these manoeuvres of the imperialists and neo-colonialists that the African journalist must be vigilant. He must shout for all the world to hear, and place on it the responsibility for thwarting their designs against Africa. The African journalist must be just as vigilant against our own faults and defections; and against our dilatoriness and unwillingness to make a reality of African unity. His is the duty to guard our African Revolution and see that it moves forward in the right direction. He must speak out, no matter the cost. His columns must vibrate with the call to the African nations to take up the challenge that the African Revolution poses.

The African Revolution has, for the most part, adopted one-party rule as its most appropriate political instrument for ending tribalism and planning development within the democratic framework of our African society. Even if we wanted it, we could not afford the deferment of strong and immediate governmental action which class and party politics entail. We cannot afford the political luxuries of capitalist democracy. We have neither the capital nor the time.

The multiplication of political parties in Western Europe has not prevented the enthronement of dictatorial powers in some countries nor political instability in others. We see the Executive of the United States constantly frustrated over its measures to end racialism and to introduce social security legislation. What can go on there for decades, without a political breakdown, would bring chaos and disaster within a short time in any African state.

That is why Ghana has chosen the way of peoples' socialist parliamentary democracy. We are aware that the one-party system cannot function in an environment contained by restrictions of a client or a neo-colonialist state. We have also chosen the path of socialism for our economic reconstruction, because we believe that it is the only way to liquidate the remnants of colonialism. We believe that it is the only sure way, and the quickest, to build a happy life for the masses of our people.

Unless Africa embraces socialism, it will move backward instead of forward. Under any other system our progress can only be slow. Our people will lose their patience. They want to see progress, and socialism is the only means that will bring it speedily. Congo Brazzavile and Dahomey are object lessons for us. The attempt to enforce a one-party system in a non-socialist environment can lead only to disaster.

Because we want strong and yet democratic governments in our African Revolution, we must guard against the dangers inherent in governments whose only opposition to tyranny and abuse lies in the folds of the ruling party itself. A ceaseless flow of self-criticism, an unending vigilance against tyranny and nepotism and other forms of bribery and corruption, unswerving loyalty to principles approved by the masses of the people, these are the main safeguards for the people under one-party rule.

Who is best able to exercise that vigilance, to furnish the material for self-criticism, to sound warnings against any departure from principles, if not the press of Revolutionary Africa?

The African press has a vital part to play in the revolution which is now sweeping over the continent. Our newspapers, our broadcasting, our information services, our television, must reach out to the masses of our people—to the workers, the farmers, the trade unionists and peasants, to the university students, the young and the old—to explain the meaning and purpose of the fight against colonialism, imperialism and neo-colonialism. It must explain the necessity for, and the meaning and purpose of, a Union Government of Africa.

Our press must be foremost in inspiring and educating the masses of our continent so that they can withstand the onslaught of decadent ideas and influences that permeate the ranks of the opportunist and neo-colonialist agents among us.

If we are to banish colonialism completely from our continent, every African must be made aware of his part in the struggle. This is the kind of education which the African press can and must help to spread.

You have a noble cause—I would say a holy cause: to work unstintingly, unhesitatingly, and fearlessly for the equality of all our people in this continent for the universality of man's rights everywhere on this globe.

Yours is the responsibility to be ever on the alert for truth and to use it without fear or favour in the noble task of forwarding total independence in Africa.

You, by your calling, have the responsibility to work unceasingly for the unity of Africa, the single means by which we can promote the prosperity of this continent and defend it against the machinations of our enemies. By reason of your chosen work, you men and women of the press are in that most vital of positions where you can persuade men's minds, inform their opinions and point the way to go. Unless you use it for good, you betray your calling, you mislead those who look to you for truth, who expect from you an interpretation of that truth in their cause.

The conclusions that you reach at this conference must sustain this position. They should assist in the speedy realisation of a union government of Africa. They should keep you in that place which no journalist should ever vacate—the vanguard of the march to freedom.

I therefore charge you to lead the final triumphant march of continent towards our unity which no imperialist or neo-colonialists will ever again be able to assail.

I wish you every success.

28

TRIBUTE TO THE LATE PRESIDENT JOHN F. KENNEDY

November 25, 1963

It is with deep sorrow that I speak to you today, and pay tribute to the memory of the late President John F. Kennedy, a great world statesman and a relentless fighter for equality and human dignity.

The whole world has been shocked and bewildered at President Kennedy's tragic death by assassination, in the prime of his life. In spite of his brief term of office, President Kennedy has made an indelible mark on the history of our time. He will be remembered as a distinguished champion for peace and the rights of man. His inspiration, his tremendous courage, his integrity and the warmth of his feeling for his fellow men will be a beacon to those who share his convictions and inspirations.

John Kennedy's achievements in international affairs have been remarkable. We in Africa will remember him, above all, for his uncompromising stand against racial and religious bigotry, intolerance and injustice. His courage and steadfastness in pursuing the objectives of racial equality in his own country will always remain as his greatest contribution to the struggle against racialism and racial arrogance. His singleness of purpose toward these objectives may have been a cause of his ignominious assassination. Whatever the cause, I am convinced that the supreme sacrifice which he was called upon to make, will not be lost on those sections of American society whose outmoded attitudes and prejudices constitute a blot on the American image.

By his death, the world has witnessed the evil manoeuvres of imperialism, capitalism and racialism. Let us hope that John Kennedy's death will shame the racialist and reactionary bigots in America into a more enlightened outlook on the problems of peace and social injustice.

President Kennedy was a remarkable man and a man of his century. Born into wealth, he was yet deeply sensitive to the problems and hopes of the common man and of the under-privileged. This aspect of his character was reflected both in his domestic and international policies.

His ideas on economic aid, social welfare and world peace were far in advance of large sections of influential opinion in his own country. As the youngest President ever of the United States, he was truly a representative of our century—a century of expanding opportunities for all, the elimination of poverty, ignorance and disease, and the establishment of a new order of truth, equality and social justice.

With a true sense of history, John Kennedy carried on, in a most dramatic manner, what Abraham Lincoln began one hundred years ago; like Lincoln, he was prevented from carrying his endeavours to the great heights he had set for himself, by an assassin's bullet. As a man endowed with great human warmth, his relationship with people was always friendly and sincere. I was privileged to meet President Kennedy and his wife in Washington in 1961, not long after he became President of the United States.

In fact, I think I am right in saying that I was the first Head of State to whom he granted audience immediately after he had been sworn in as the President of the United States.

I was deeply impressed by his wisdom and sincerity. His presence—his sense of understanding and appreciation of the grave issues confronting our world, and his genuine interest in the solution of the problems confronting developing countries made me regard him, even then, as a man from whom the world could expect great things, as a man who could become one of the most important leaders of our time.

It really takes a man like John Kennedy to say—and I quote from his writings:

"A man does what he must in spite of personal consequences, in spite of obstacles and dangers and pressure—and that is the basis of all human morality."

We in Africa can have no more appropriate epitaph to John Kennedy's memory than his own words spoken in his inaugural address:-

"...whether you are citizens of America or of the world, ask of us the same high standards of strength and sacrifice that we shall ask of you. With a good conscience our only sure wards, with history the final judge of our deeds, let us go forth to lead the land we love, asking His blessing and His help, but knowing that here on earth God's work must truly be our own."

To his dear wife and children, I send deepest condolences on my own behalf and on behalf of the People of Ghana.

Osagyefo the President has sent the following message to President Lyndon B. Johnson, President of the United States of America:-

"I am bewildered and shocked at the tragic news of the assassination of my personal friend and great statesman, John F. Kennedy. President Kennedy was a distinguished champion in the great fight for the rights of man. It needed a man of President Kennedy's courage to take the uncompromising stand which characterised his policies for the achievement of racial equality and human dignity. By his notable achievements during his unexpectedly brief term of office President Kennedy left a profound mark on the course of human history. May his supreme sacrifice fortify men of goodwill to redouble their efforts towards the achievement of justice, freedom, equality and the brotherhood of man. Please accept on behalf of myself, the Government and people of Ghana profound condolences on this great loss."

TO: MRS. JOHN F. KENNEDY

"I have received with profound shock and distress the news of the assassination of your beloved husband and my great friend. By his death the world has lost a wise and courageous statesman whose contribution to the maintenance of world peace and security and whose uncompromising stand for human rights and dignity will long be remembered. Please accept my deepest sympathy in your bereavement and may God grant you strength and fortitude in this hour of tribulation."

THE ACADEMY OF SCIENCES DINNER

November 30, 1963

First of all, I would like to welcome all those who have come from overseas to take part in our anniversary celebration, many of whom are old friends. We are also glad to have other guests among us, who are no strangers to me. In particular I would like to say how appreciative we are to Sir William Slater for accepting our invitation to come and give this year's anniversary address, and for having chosen a topic so stimulating and so appropriate—appropriate because we are embarking on a real agricultural and industrial revolution in this country. Our Seven-Year Plan, which will soon be published and launched, is keyed to the development of our industry and agriculture. I hope that all of you who have come to join us in these celebrations will enjoy your visit.

Most people usually expect after-dinner speeches to be made in a somewhat light and frivolous vein. But at a dinner for an Academy of Sciences, surrounded as I am by so many serious-minded scholars, scientists and research workers, I hesitate to treat you to the trite remarks that characterize after-dinner speeches. On the other hand, I don't want you to feel like the Mathematician-Scientist who breathlessly burst into a room, shouting excitedly: "Minus four, minus three, minus two, minus one—I've done it! I've recited the negative numbers!"

It is fitting on this Fourth Anniversary of the Academy of Sciences, that we should consider how far we have been able to carry out our objectives and make our plans accordingly for the future development of the Academy.

The Academy of Sciences, as we know it to-day, is the result of a happy merger between the Academy of Learning and the National Research Council. Many of you here will recall that both these institutions were inaugurated by the Duke of Edinburgh during his visit in Ghana in 1959. At my request, the Duke of Edinburgh accepted the invitation to become President of the Ghana Academy of Learning for the first two years of its existence. In his inaugural address the Duke stated that if the Academy carried out its duties and functions with enlightenment and integrity, it would not be long before its influence was felt throughout Ghana and, indeed, throughout Africa. This challenge applies with equal force to the Ghana Academy of Sciences which has replaced these two institutions. We are determined to fulfil that prophecy.

The National Research Council, the second parent of the Academy of Sciences, was established by us in the determination that scientific research should take its proper place in our country's development.

Recently, however, we felt that the then existing situation in which the Ghana Academy of Learning and the National Research Council operated separately was unsatisfactory. There was too much duplication of effort. The two bodies were complementary to each other, in that while the National Research Council was responsible for the more practical research programmes, the Academy of Learning was engaged mainly in fundamental research.

We decided that better results would be achieved if these two bodies were joined together in a common endeavour.

The Academy of Sciences was created, therefore, as a new and dynamic body to assume full responsibility for the co-ordination of all aspects of research and the promotion of scientific pursuits and learning. In this way, we have combined in one institution the fundamental academic functions originally envisaged for the Academy of Learning and the applied scientific research so vital for our national development. We expect that from this amalgamation will grow the strength and power which will push us faster in the development of the sciences and literary arts.

We do not however conceive the functions of the Academy as passive, or as the mere collection and compilation of date from our universities and research institutions. The Academy is expected to design and carry out research programmes, related to the life, changes and growth of our society. For this reason, the Academy has under it about twenty Research Institutes among which are the National Institute of Health and Medical Research, the Cocoa Research Institute at Tafo, the Building Research Institute at Kumasi and the Agricultural Research Institute at Kwadaso. There is even a research project attached to the Academy which is doing vigorous research into Ghanaian herbal and botanic medicine and natural therapies.

It is in these Institutes that the Academy, assisted by a team of competent scientists and research workers, is tackling some of the problems of pure and applied science in Ghana.

We expect that those who have been elected as Fellows of the Academy will justify their selection by their work and by assisting in the solution of some of the many problems facing us in both applied and pure research. Facilities have been made available in our Universities for Fellows to carry out their work. I would suggest, in this connection, that an annual register should be kept showing the work in progress and the work completed by Fellows. We believe not only in pure research as a legitimate endeavour, but we also attach great importance to applied research. Modern science has taught us enough, and has already given us enough, to be able to tackle our agricultural, industrial and economic problems. Modern science has taught us enough to be able to assist us in solving the practical problems of education, agriculture, medicine, engineering and industry.

There is no need for us to go through all the long and complicated stages of the development of science which other countries have gone through in the past. We are, as it were, jumping the centuries, using the knowledge and experience already available to us. What others have taken hundreds of years to do, we must achieve in a generation. It is useless to say that we must move through the stages of coal, oil and gas to electricity Ghana is already in the era of electricity. We have jumped from coal and kerosene to electricity within a generation. We are now face to face with Atomic energy.

Ladies and Gentlemen: The Academy can and must accept a positive and active role in the life and development of our nation.

A full-size Secretariat has been established in the Academy, and its existence must facilitate the work and the expansion of the institutes directly concerned with research. The Academy must show initiative in identifying research problems and in suggesting research priorities of national significance.

It is not possible to talk of the uses of science nowadays without our enthusiasm being dampened by the use to which science has been put for baneful purposes. I have many times stressed the fact that humanity has a vested interest in peace. The loss of peace in modern times would mean the same as the end of humanity. Except we can have the world without the bomb, or we can have the bomb without the world, but we cannot have both. Unless science is only applied for peaceful ends, the practice of science itself might soon cease. For there would be no scientist; and incidentally there would be no philosophers and politicians.

Our Academy of Sciences has already established contact with a number of Academies of Sciences in other countries. I hope that through such contacts our scientists will unite their efforts with scientists elsewhere in the positive and beneficial use of science and help to make war through science impossible on our planet.

The importance of the study of sciences in our own educational programmes cannot be emphasised enough. Our need for trained scientists of all kinds and for men with technological skill is fundamental to the socialist society which we are committed to create. Only the mastery and unremitting application of science and technology can guarantee human welfare and human happiness. Socialism without science is empty. To achieve socialism, the emphasis in our educational system must be shifted from purely literary concern to science and technology.

New polytechnics are being established in the country and existing ones are being expanded. Special arrangements have also been made for the training of science teachers with the rapidity necessary to staff our schools, colleges and institutions.

It is the aim of the Academy of Sciences to popularise the sciences and to make the mass of our people science-conscious.

It is significant here that a Science Museum will shortly be established in this country under the auspices of the Academy of Sciences and will be located in Accra. I am sure such a museum will inspire and excite interest in science and technology in both young and old. I am sure that it will help to foster a spirit of wonder and exploration in all who visit it.

Ladies and Gentlemen: A socialist society can only be maintained by people who have a correct understanding of nature, and who hold within their grasp the knowledge and the means to master and transform nature for the common good of all.

We have the resources to create a better life for our people. What we need is widespread conviction in the correctness of our ideology, the will and the effort to mobilise our intellectual, social and material resources in a dynamic effort to establish the just and the prosperous society.

It is for this reason that this Academy must not become purely honorific, a social club in which members put one another on the back when they meet and engage in endless debates and arguments. Rather, this Academy must become a vital force and the intellectual and scientific centre of the vigour of our nation, committed entirely to the purposes of our society, and bending its talents to the realisation of those purposes.

I am happy to be able to say that already a pharmaceutical chemist in the Kwame Nkrumah University of Science and Technology has succeeded in extracting from Ghanaian plants a new alkaloid which shows great possibilities of being more efficient for anaethestics than the alkaloids now used for surgical operation purposes.

But it is towards this sort of achievement, in my opinion, that our energies should be directed. I am not concerned with plans for exploring the moon, Mars or any of the other planets. They are too far from me anyway. My concern is here on earth where so much needs to be done to make it a place fit for human effort, endeavour and happiness. Science must be directed towards fighting and overcoming poverty and disease and in raising the standard of life of the people of the earth; its aims must be for the promotion of peace and, through peace, the happiness of mankind. Unless science is used for the betterment of mankind, I am at a loss to understand the reason for it at all. It does not require a clever brain to destroy life. In fact any fool can do that. But it takes brains—and extraordinarily brilliant brains—to create conditions for human happiness and to make human life worth living. The Ghana Academy of Sciences belongs to our society. It belongs to our African revolution. It is one of the valuable organs for our society, and it must work to assist and improve our general welfare. The Academy can justify its status in our society only by the contribution which it makes to the progress and development of the nation.

Political independence is only a means to an end. Its value lies in its being used to create new economic, social and cultural conditions which colonialism and imperialism have denied us for so long.

In Africa to-day, there is a general agreement that our political independence can only be safeguarded within the framework of a union government of Africa. Our scholars and scientists have a right and an obligation to assist in the creation of this African Continental Union. It is within that union alone that the African genius can thrive in complete freedom, unshackled by imperialism and neo-colonialism.

It is my hope that one day we shall see one African Academy of Sciences with the regional branches tackling the scientific problems facing us in Africa as a whole. I am convinced that the United Nations and its specialised agencies could achieve better results by working within a federal union government of Africa.

As I have said before, our need for scientists is great. It is encouraging, however; that we have an increasing number of students coming forward for further training in science and technology. Most of these students are already in our universities and polytechnics. We have also increased the number of State scholarships which will enable Ghanaians abroad to qualify in science, technology, medicine and agriculture. We have over a thousand Ghanaian students in the United Kingdom who have been awarded scholarships to enable them to complete their courses in these scientific subjects. We are extending this scholarship scheme to cover our students in America and in Europe. In addition, over a thousand Ghanaian students are pursuing various scientific studies in the Soviet Union, in China and in other socialist countries.

We can therefore look to the future with hope. Let the Ghana Academy of Science lay firm foundations for the application of science to social needs and and development. This will be an inspiration to our young men and women.

And now, Ladies and Gentlemen: I give you a toast.

A toast to the progress of the Ghana Academy of Sciences and to the Fellows of the Academy of Sciences.

A toast to the scientists and scholars all over the world.

A toast to world peace and eternal friendship among the nations and peoples of the earth.

30

INAUGURATION OF THE WORKERS' COLLEGE

December 5, 1963

I congratulate the Institute of Public Education on the inauguration of the Accra Workers' College, and on the establishment of many similar institutions throughout Ghana.

Education is recognised throughout the world as a powerful vehicle in the development of the people and of nations; it is also the most rewarding form of investment. In a rapidly developing country like Ghana, where our primary aim is to create a dynamic socialist society, conditions must be provided for the full development of the potentialities of every individual. It is fundamental, therefore, that the well-springs of knowledge should be brought within the easy reach of all. It is by this process that we hope to raise the standard of education of the average maul and woman of Ghana.

It is equally important that through education, we should improve the welfare of the people and enable every person not only to play an effective role in the economic, cultural, technological and scientific revolution of our time, but also make his personal contribution to our struggle for the freedom and unity of the African continent.

The Institute of Public Education and the Workers' Colleges in all parts of Ghana have a vital role to play in the national drive to make education available to all. With the establishment of these Colleges, we hope to see a large and virile body of students among the workers, dedicated to the pursuit of learning not merely for it own sake, but for the improvement of our society and to enable us people to understand clearly what is going on in the world around them. Only thus can we equip ourselves to recognise and resist the machinations of imperialism and neo-colonialism.

Our Workers' Colleges must help to eradicate, as quickly as possible, all forms of inequality of opportunity in our society. Let all workers, the men and women of Ghana, young and old, therefore, make the fullest use of the facilities available at these Colleges, and help to increase our national productivity, enhance the prosperity and the character of our nation, and uphold the dignity of the African Personality.

MESSAGE TO U THANT
U.N. SECRETARY GENERAL

Office of the President
December 16, 1963

MY DEAR SECRETARY-GENERAL,

Is there any need to stress to you what the independence of the Congo must mean to every African leader who regards the freedom and prosperity of the whole African continent as individual? But even for those who think in national, sectional or regional terms, any form of foreign control over the Congo Republic constitutes an immediate and substantial threat to their own independence.

Geographically, strategically and politically, the Congo is the most vital region of Africa. Military control of the Congo by any foreign power would give it easy access to most of the continent South of the Sahara.

Geographically, it owes its importance not only to its central position, but to its vast area and tremendous resources. Although these resources have hardly been tapped, they have already enriched foreign interests to a degree which has made them adamant to continue with the exploitation of the Congo's wealth, and has aroused the cupidity of others to share in this exploitation.

The strategic importance of the Congo derives from its geographical features. Foreign Powers which have concerned themselves with what they like to call "the defence of Africa"—by which they mean the defence, on the African continent, of interests which are mainly contrary to those of the African people—clearly regard the Congo as the key to the military control of Africa. This is the significance of the aid which Belgium received from her allies to build great military bases at Kitona in the West and Kamina in the East of the Congo. This is the reason why there are eight international airports, thirty principal and over a hundred secondary and local airports in the Congo.

The Congo represents "strategic space" to Western military and civilian experts when considering the likelihood of a war with their enemies from bases in Africa. The size and pivotal position of the Congo furnish the greatest military advantages, either for the purpose of attack or defence when fighting in Africa. In the geographical theories of men like Mackinder and Haushofer, the Congo is the area from which the domination of Africa can be ensured, and this assumption is shared by leading political scientists who do not necessarily agree with all the geo-political theories. There is a concensus of opinion among Western strategists that the Congo must be in hands friendly to the West. This can mean nothing else in the final analysis, but that the West must have control over the Government of the Congo. If the Soviet Union had made such a claim over the Congo, we would be justified in accusing it of seeking to drag the Congo into the defence system of the Eastern Bloc. We do not want to bring the Cold War into Africa. The Congo should be independent and neutral—it should be absolutely free and sovereign, and should not be controlled by either the East or the West.

In fact this is precisely what the West has now achieved in the Congo. The Central Government is constrained to believe that its interests coincide with Western interests. The future is not even left in such uncertain hands. The future is ensured by seeing to it that the Congolese Army, although theoretically under the Central Government, is in fact managed principally by two Western Powers through the so-called "Binza Group."

For military planners and economic exploiters alike, the fact that a Government subservient to foreign Powers can only perpetuate the present misery, stagnation and disorder of the people of the Congo, while reserving far greater horror for them in the event of war, is unfortunately a matter of indifference.

The political importance of the Congo is, of course, closely related to its strategic and economic importance. This combined importance must attract military intervention, as well as all the subtler forms practiced in all Independent African States where foreign interests seek to retain their former colonial privileges.

The Congo is not only politically important because of its vast resources and strategic space in the event of a global or continental war, but because it is the buffer state between independent Africa in

North, and the territories of colonialism and white supremacy in the South. Northwards stands free Africa determined on a free continent. Southwards, Angola begins and stretches to the stronghold of colonial and racial oppression, the Republic of South Africa.

It will require not only the most pervasive system of foreign intrigue, but direct intervention to prevent the Congolese people from coming to the aid of their brothers in Angola fighting for freedom. They have made and continue to make heavy sacrifices toward this end.

It will require not only a Congo vitiated and corrupted by neo-colonialism, but a hostile Congolese Government openly siding with colonialism and supremacy, to prevent independent Africa from using the Congo as a corridor and a base for all possible aid to the peoples of Angola and Southern Africa fighting for their liberation.

Thus, the degree of the Congo's independence will substantially determine the ultimate fate of the whole Continent of Africa. Free Africa will never abandon its struggle to end colonialism and to expel white supremacy from the whole continent. An independent Congo will be unreservedly on Africa's side in that struggle whilst Congo, with a Government controlled by imperialism and neo-colonialism, because of its geographical position, will be assisting Portuguese colonialism and South African apartheid even by playing a neutral or semi-passive role.

The South African Republic, Portugal and the settler regime of Southern Rhodesia are well aware of the Congo's strategic and political importance. This accounted for their open and constant support for the Tshombe secessionist regime in the Katanga, even at the risk of colliding with the forces of the United Nations. The colonialist alliance, for the same reasons, cannot cease from intervening in the Congo affairs now, from undermining the Congo's stability and from urging their friends in the West to maintain control over the Congo's Government. Secession, disruption and neo-colonialist control in the Congo are considered essential political aims by the colonial territories in Southern Africa.

These reasons amply suffice to show why, and in what sense, Congo. Sections of the press in some of these countries have even had the effrontery to rebuke us, leaders of Independent African states, for our efforts to sustain the independence of the Congo.

Thus, when I wrote letters of advice to the Late Patrice Lumumba, this press raised the cry that this constituted interference in the international affairs of the Congo; but when the tools and thugs of the Union Miniere murdered the same Patrice Lumumba, no one in these quarters referred to that as interference in the internal affairs of the Congo. One newspaper, with a very large circulation in the city of New York, could find no other comment than the word: "Another Red Gone to Hell." For, of course, all this conspiracy against the Congo is carried on under the banner of anti- Communism. Lumumba was not killed because he was thought to be a Communist; but because he was a nationalist leader threatening the monopolies of the Union Miniere. It was for that reason that all who wished to keep the Congo weak, subservient and divided became his enemies, and for that reason that, even today, those in the Congo who sincerely hold to his principles and convictions are persecuted and imprisoned.

We are now approaching another turning point in the history of the Congo. The United Nations forces, sooner or later, will have to withdraw. The question is: what will follow that withdrawal? Will there be, at the behest of outside influences, a military coup, with General Mobutu, or someone in a similar position, taking over power, and perhaps with the return of Moise Tshombe, the puppet of the Union Miniere, to a position of influence? There are indications that preparations are being made for such an outcome, which would turn the Congo back into a colony in all but name. What is the significance, for example, of the retraining programme which has been announced for the Congolese Army? This programme is placed in the hands of a group of NATO countries and their allies. At present, Congolese paratroopers are being trained by Israeli Air Force personnel and the ground Forces by some hundred Belgian Army Officers. This is a very strange programme indeed for a non-aligned country, and the Congo, from the formation of the Adoula Government in July, 1961, has declared itself to be non-aligned country. M. Adoula and M. Gizenga, indeed, attended together the Conference of the non-aligned countries at Belgrade. M. Gizenga is now in captivity and M. Adoula has allowed NATO to take over the training of his Army. I cannot believe M. Adoula would have committed himself to such a course, in clear contradiction with his, declared policy of non-alignment, were he a free agent. The sad fact is that in Leopoldville now, as at all times since the betrayal and downfall of Patrice Lumumba, the dominant interests are those of a group of Western Powers. We have sympathy for M. Adoula in this very difficult situation, but can we consider him to be speaking for the Congolese people while he remains politically and militarily dependent on outside powers?

Even when M. Adoula makes a token assertion of the independence by allowing the AGIP Oil Company to operate in the Congo in competition with the existing American and Belgian Companies, his position as Prime Minister is openly threatened.

The fact is that nothing and nobody can help the Congolese people to free themselves unless the African nations come to their help in unity and in accordance with the spirit of Addis Ababa. The African nations must insist that the United Nations force in the Congo shall be an All-African one, under African Command; that it should be this force, and not NATO, which should be in charge of the retraining programme for the Congolese Army, and that this programme should include the stamping out of bribery and corruption and the removal of officers who are working as agents for foreign powers.

In order that the Congolese people and their representatives shall be able to express their wishes freely, the first step necessary is the reorganisation of the Army, placing it on such a footing that it can no longer be used as a tool of foreign interests or employed for the terrorising, imprisoning and murder of patriots. The NATO retraining programme will not secure these ends; indeed, it will secure precisely the opposition of those ends because officers who are "pro-NATO"—that is to say, who are prepared to serve foreign countries rather than their own—will be placed in key positions. This will perpetuate all the evils which have afflicted the Congo. The only thing, therefore, which can save the Congo is the kind of programme I have described. Technically, such a programme is perfectly possible. The obstacles in the way are not technical but political, arising from the conception which certain Western Powers have of their interests in the Congo—a conception which, I believe, must in the long run end in disaster.

I must urge you, Mr. Secretary-General, to use your great office, for the sake of the African people and in the interests of World peace, to set in motion consultative machinery for replacing the military forces of the United Nations by an All-African Force under the provisions of the Addis Ababa Charter, as soon as the period of the present mandate of the United Nations expires.

Yours sincerely,

KWAME NKRUMAH

President, Republic of Ghana.

32

LAYING OF THE FOUNDATION STONE AT THE PRE-FABRICATED CONCRETE PANEL FACTORY

October 16, 1963

This factory for pre-fabricated building elements, the foundation stone of which we are laying this afternoon, is a concrete realisation of the efforts that have been made by the Party and the Government to build houses for the people, particularly the workers of Ghana. The workers and people of Ghana should acclaim this as the beginning of the end of the housing shortage in the country.

Since our Party came into power, our concern for houses for the people has never diminished. You will all remember the Schokbeton Housing Scheme, the Swedish Timber Houses we introduced and the ups and downs of the Ghana Housing Corporation in the provision of Estate Houses. All these attempts have had one aim: to provide houses for the people. And here, at long last, we have a factory which will help to expedite the solution of this vital need.

When this factory is completed, we shall manufacture here, in large numbers, pre-fabricated structures which will be used for the construction of dwelling houses, flats and other buildings and thus assist and accelerate the efforts we are making to provide houses and homes for all.

When this factory comes into operation in about a year from now, it will be possible to build room units at the rate of 1,000 a day, at reasonable cost and within the reach of the average person in Ghana. Plans have already been completed for the construction of residential areas in Kaneshie and in Tema. We propose, in this connection, to provide dwelling houses for more than 22,000 workers in Accra, and 11,000 in Tema. These residential estates will comprise four-storey blocks of flats, schools, clinics, shops, community centres, and playing grounds for the children who will live in the estates.

We are painfully aware of the needs of the people throughout Ghana for adequate housing.

Already much has been done to meet this demand. The record of the Government in providing houses for the people has not been bad at all. By the end of last year, the Ghana Housing Corporation had constructed over 2,000 units of accommodation in the urban areas throughout Ghana. The First Ghana Building Society to which Government has made generous grants had granted loans totalling over £G1 million to nearly 600 people for the purchase and construction of their own houses. In addition, the Government Roof Loan Schemes have granted loans up to £G1½ million by the end of 1962 mainly in the rural areas. Under this Scheme, more than 11,000 houses of improved quality have been built throughout our towns and villages.

This year alone, the Ghana Housing Corporation has built 200 houses in the principal towns throughout the country. Another 200 more are under construction.

Only recently, the Government has voted a sum of £G100,000 to enable the Housing Corporation to provide houses for those who lost their homes in the Cape Coast area. This factory will enable us to do far more in this direction. This factory will help us to achieve our objective of housing the people. In Ghana the son of man will have a place to lay his head.

In the Party Programme for Work and Happiness we have recognised the fundamental right of everyone living in Ghana to adequate housing for himself and his family. Our aim, therefore, is to see that everyone whether he is a civil servant, a teacher, a farmer, a carpenter, a clerk, a market woman or an ordinary worker—can, if he so wishes acquire a decent house or flat to live in at a reasonable rate and without difficulty or too much red tape.

By the construction of this factory, we shall be able to improve the living conditions of the workers throughout Ghana.

And here I would like to extend my appreciation to the Soviet Government for agreeing to assist us in establishing this factory. It is really a people's factory. When I was in the Soviet Union, I personally spoke to Comrade Khrushchev about our housing problems. Out of the discussion we had, we are to-day laying the foundation of this housing factory.

And so, in friendship between the Government of the Soviet Union and Ghana, I declare the foundation stone of this factory well and truly laid.

CHRISTMAS MESSAGE

Accra
December 24, 1963

I wish to send you all, wherever you may be, my warmest greetings and very best wishes for your happiness and well-being at this Christmas time. And may your thoughts be with our Nation at this time also.

Fellow countrymen, the events happening around us compel us to think seriously about the happiness and welfare of our country and to re-dedicate ourselves to the ideals for which we stand. Let us close our ranks in devoted service to one another. As we enjoy ourselves, let us think of the happiness of our neighbours.

This year has seen the consolidation of our efforts to create a new society and to promote a better life for all of you. Let us draw inspiration from our achievements and continue to work for the realisation of all the things which bring happiness. Let us renew our faith in the future by applying, in our daily lives, the universal message of Christmas, and devote ourselves to the service and well-being of our fellow men. Christmas will have no meaning for us if we fail to listen to its great appeal to the innate goodness in us all.

What is my wish for you and our Nation this Christmas Season? If you ask me this, in sincerity, I will say: Countrymen, let us move forward together as one man to our destiny, with courage and steadfastness all the way, proud of our past and confident about our future.

Countrymen, I am today completing the action started by the National Assembly yesterday in connection with the recent treason trial. In the exercise of the powers conferred upon me by the National, Assembly, I have to-day declared all the proceedings and the judgement of the recent treason trial as of no effect whatsoever. In other words, the judgement of the Special Court is declared null and void.

Have a good rest, and enjoy yourselves at Christmas time. Many of you will travel outside your usual place of work. I ask you to be careful on the roads. Ghana, your Government and I need everyone of you in the great tasks ahead.

Once, again, I wish you all a very happy Christmas.

34

NEW YEAR'S MESSAGE

Accra
December 31, 1963

I have come to the microphone this evening, on the eve of the New Year, to share a few thoughts with you and to wish each and everyone of you a Happy and Prosperous New Year.

Much has been accomplished in the year that is about to pass away. By any standards, we have every reason to be thankful for all the great changes that have taken place in our country. In all, our policy can be summed up in a single sentence: to achieve a higher living standard by improving the living conditions of our people, and providing increased opportunities for employment, and to assist in the total freedom and unity of Africa within the framework of a continental Union Government.

Nearly seven years ago, when Ghana became independent, there were only seven other independent African states. Today, that number has risen to thirty-four. In 1964 when Northern Rhodesia and Nyasaland become independent, there will, in all, be thirty-six independent states in Africa. Practically, the whole of Northern and Central Africa will thus have emerged from colonialism. The unfreed part of our continent is fighting relentlessly to be free, and it will not be long, with the passing of 1963 and the coming in of 1964, when all Africa will be free and united.

Indeed, as I speak to you now, in a few hours, the imperialist-imposed Central African Federation would have come to an end. This is surely a great victory for the Liberation Movement so courageously sustained by the African Liberation Movement.

In the international field, all we ask for is that every effort will be made to bring about a relaxation of tension and the end of the Cold War. In any event, we insist that the Cold War should be kept out of Africa. Surely, the expectation which we held for Africa on the eve of our own independence, namely, that the independence of Ghana will have no meaning except in the context of the total liberation of Africa, is now almost realised. But the final victory will lie in the political unification of Africa, free from foreign control, manipulation and dominations.

It is not enough to acclaim unity. We must work conscientiously and tirelessly for its attainments. All the evils that beset us in Africa: economic exploitation, boundary disputes, the existence of foreign bases on African soil, the intrigues, bribery, subversion, and cajolement of neo-colonialism, poverty, and want amidst plenty—all these evils that are the legacy of colonialism and imperialism can only be effectively removed if we unite under one Union Government o Africa.

I hope that 1964 will see a positive advance towards our goal of African unity.

At home, we continue to spend a greater proportion of our revenue on education than perhaps any other country in the world. This in itself, is a great investment for the future. Our system of education must therefore be such as to equip our youth for the Socialist reconstruction of Ghana. We are building factories and providing employment for the people. We are going through an industrial and agricultural revolution. We are moving irresistibly out of the one-crop economy and approaching the portals of a diversified agriculture economy. Above all, the Volta River Project is edging its way into our future with its limitless promise for industrialisation and prosperity.

I could go on enlarging on the benefits which have come to us in the way of better housing and the rising standards of living during the past years; but that is not my intention at this moment. I wish rather to lay stress on what we could advance, and have not progressed.

A revolutionary people, with a revolutionary Party, working at a revolutionary tempo, and with faith in its revolution, can move mountains. Our human and natural resources in Ghana are sufficient; to transform our country speedily into an industrialised and prosperous state. So far, we have not mobilised or utilised our resources to the limits of our power. We are united, but we are not yet working as hard as we should.

That is not because there is no dedication or vision in us as a people, but because we do not make calls on ourselves.

In a few weeks from now I shall launch our Seven-year Development Plan. The Plan will demand from party members, from our administrators, from our civil servants, from our workers and farmers, from our managers of state enterprises, from our organisations and institutions, from our Magistrates and Judges, from our University Professors and Students, from our Doctors and all other professional men and women Teachers and Scientists—indeed, from each and everyone of you, the greatest sacrifice and dedication.

If we prove to be old wine in new bottles we shall fail to arouse the enthusiasm and spirit of our people. If we become self-satisfied, and allow ourselves to be bound by tradition, precedent and habit, or if we allow the apathy of a few people in key positions to slow down our progress, we shall be undermining the spirit of our revolution.

It is never easy to determined in a State like ours, freed recently from colonial rule and domination, and burdened with the remnants of colonialist indoctrination and contradictions, how many secret enemies and hidden agents departing colonialists have left behind in our midst. We are better off if we can trust one another rather than engender an atmosphere of mutual suspicion. Yet, unless we exercise the utmost vigilance and mete out the heaviest punishments for treachery and subversion, our revolution is always in danger of being undermined.

Let us, then, follow a few simple roles of vigilance, justice and fairplay in the coming year. Let us not be taken in by those who play lip-service to our cause. Let us watch out carefully for anti-socialist behaviour, whether it takes the form of outright deception or sabotage. We must be quick to expose and to punish bribery and corruption, and misuse of State property.

In quarters where Government decisions are delayed and frustrated, we must find out who are responsible, and caution or discipline them. We should examine ourselves critically in relation to the Community in which we live and see how we can help to arrest the evils and shortcomings that exist in our society. Your behaviour must inspire others and not breed cynicism and apathy with practices completely at variance with our Socialist endeavours and aspirations. If we do this, we have no reason to look forward to anything but greater economic and cultural victories and the enhancement of spiritual and moral values in the coming year.

For certain historic reasons, the eyes of Africa are turned upon us in hope and confidence, whilst the eyes of the imperialists and neo-colonialists glare at us with hostility. Every victory for our advance will be a new impetus for Africa; every failure will be a cause of rejoicing in the imperialist camp. In this struggle, we can neither spare ourselves nor the opponents and enemies of our revolution.

Men and women of Ghana, I now wish to turn to the recent treason trial and the situation created by the judgement of the Special Court. As you already know, I have, in exercise of the powers conferred upon me by Parliament, declared the judgement null and void.

May I, however, make one point clear: The President appoints the Chief Justice, the Judges of the Supreme Court and the Judges of the High Court. In the performance of their duties Judges are not interferred with by the Chief Executive and, to this extent, they exercise the judicial powers of the State independent of the Executive.

But, under our Constitution the office of the Chief Justice is not solely judicial. It is also quasi-political. It involves active co-operation and understanding with the President in securing justice, law and order, peace and stability. In other words, the position of the Chief Justice of Ghana is such that the holder of the post must be conscious of his political responsibility.

A treason trial, by its very nature, is political and can lead to unrest, disturbances and even violence. For this reason, our Government was bound to be interested in the treason trial by virtue of the fact that it is the responsibility of the Government to maintain law and order and to ensure the security of the State.

The failure of the Chief Justice to take the President into his confidence in regard to the judgement of the Special Court showed a serious disregard for the office of the President. His failure also to recognise the effect that the judgement, whatever it was, would have on the peace, stability and order throughout the country, for which the Government would be responsible, was a clear indication of his lack of political responsibility.

The Judges of the Special Court, by their failure to take me into their confidence, meant to create discontent and terror throughout the county. You the people of Ghana have made me the conscience of the Nation. My duty is not only to govern but to ease the conscience of the people by giving them peace of mind and tranquility. The Nation cannot tolerate a dishonest and corrupt judiciary. I want to assure you all that there is a possibility of a re-trail of the persons involved in this particular case, depending upon the results of certain investigations now in progress.

In the circumstances, the Government, in the interest of the people, wishes to take advantage of the situation created by the judgement in the treason trial to make certain amendments to our Constitution.

I and the Government have therefore decided that a referendum should be held between the 24th of January and 31st of January next year (1964) to seek approval of the people for the amendment of the Constitution in the following respect:-

1. To invest the President with power in his discretion to remove a Judge of the Supreme Court at any time for reasons which appear to him sufficient. The powers of Parliament to remove a Judge of the Supreme Court or a Judge of the High Court from office by resolution on grounds of stated misbehaviour or infirmity of body or mind will remain unchanged

2. To provide that in conformity with the interests, welfare and aspirations of the people, and in order to develop the organisational initiative and political activity of the people there shall be one National Party in Ghana, which shall be the vanguard of our people in their struggle to build a Socialist society and which shall be the leading core of all organisations of the people.

3. That the one National Party shall be the Convention People's Party.

The details of the Referendum will be announced soon.

The Government and I have also decided to make legislation to provide for a new national flag, the colours of which shall be the same as those of the Convention People's Party, red, white, and green—with the black star in the middle.

Friends countrymen,

We are a young and vigorous nation, dedicated to the building of a Socialist society: with socialism, we shall be able to promote rapidly, the economic growth of our country, and raise the living standards of our people. All we mean here is that the ownership of the major means of production and distribution should be vested in the State, that is in the people.

This demands that we must all work to achieve production that can satisfy the growing material, cultural and spiritual needs and requirements of our people.

The Convention People's Party has been the vanguard of our struggle all along. Nearly fifteen years ago we put our trust in our great Party and gave it the mandate to fight for independence. Under its banner, we fought against the seemingly impregnable forces of colonialism and imperialism and won. Let us resolve in the new year to continue the struggle against the enemies of our independence —against indolence, against dishonesty, against greed, against subversion, against bribery, against corruption, and against all those evils which militate against the interest and welfare of our people.

I know, and I am confident, that in the spirit of dedication and resolve we shall win yet greater victories in the years ahead.

And now, before I leave the microphone, may I wish each and everyone of you Health, Happiness and Success in the New Year.

www.ingramcontent.com/pod-product-compliance
Lightning Source LLC
Chambersburg PA
CBHW021829300426
44114CB00009BA/382